WILDLIFE
TRAVELLER
SCOTTISH
MAINLAND

The author and publisher have made every effort to ensure that the information in this publication is accurate, and accept no responsibility whatsoever for any loss, injury or inconvenience experienced by any person or persons whilst using this book.

published by
pocket mountains ltd
6 Church Wynd, Bo'ness EH51 0AN
www.pocketmountains.com

ISBN: 0-9550822-3-4
EAN: 978-0-95508-223-8

Photography copyright © Richard Rowe. Additional photography copyright © Chris Gomarsall/RSPB Images, page: 47; Peter Cairns/www.northshots.com, pages: 49, 51, 67, 69, 73, 83, 89; David Leaver/www.guideliner.co.uk, page: 57; Laurie Campbell, pages: 15, 75; Charlie Phillips, page: 77

The right of Richard Rowe to be identified as the Author of this work has been asserted by him in accordance with the Copyright, Designs and Patents Act 1988

A catalogue record for this book is available from the British Library

Printed in Poland

Introduction

Scotland is renowned for its dramatic scenery, but the wildlife that inhabits it is rather less familiar. For a small country, Scotland contains a diverse mix of habitat that in turn supports an enviable array of plants and animals – often in prolific numbers.

This guide contains 40 wildlife destinations on the Scottish mainland, journeying from the south of Scotland up through the Grampian Highlands to Cape Wrath in the far north.

Classic Scottish species such as red deer, pine marten and golden eagle are all present, but so too are vast numbers of wintering and breeding birds and a high density of otters. Scotland also holds Europe's largest population of seals, while several of the 20 or so species of cetacean (whales, dolphins and porpoises) recorded in Scottish waters are relatively common.

Destinations in this guide have been chosen to reflect the variety of habitat found in each area and its relevance to particular wildlife. Some animals are easily seen, while others require more patience – and understanding.

Many of the destinations are reserves managed by charities and agencies such as the RSPB and Scottish Natural Heritage (SNH) and are easily enjoyed by all. Others involve more rugged expeditions, some with brief boat rides.

A car can serve as an ideal 'hide' when viewing wary species or those that are vulnerable to disturbance. But where possible and conditions allow, visitors are encouraged to embrace the spirit of adventure inherent in Scotland's wild places by exploring on foot, by bike or from the water.

Visitors can minimise their impact on the environment, and maintain good relations with local inhabitants, by keeping to purpose-built paths where they exist, restricting the use of bikes to tracks, parking sensibly and avoiding fires and litter. Sadly, dogs and wildlife do not mix: check locally and use common sense. And always use a lead when around grazing land and during lambing.

How to use this guide

The destinations in this guide are divided into five regions, starting in the south. The opening section introduces the key features of each area, together with a regional map. Brief access information and a relevant Ordnance Survey (OS) map for detailed navigation are provided at the beginning of individual location entries.

Many of the RSPB, SNH and other managed reserves have information centres and good trail maps onsite, while staff are often available to answer questions. In more remote locations, it is worth checking in local shops or tourist information centres for details on guided walks and wildlife sightings.

Responsible wildlife watching

The growing popularity of wildlife-based tourism has lengthened the traditional season in Scotland, bringing jobs and visitors to remote communities well into shoulder periods. It has also spawned a growth in land- and marine-based wildlife tour operators. Most are highly professional and follow strict codes of conduct. For your own enjoyment, and the sake of the wildlife you hope to see, these are the operators you should book with.

For guidance, members of Wild Scotland – an association of wildlife tourism operators – adhere to a charter that puts wildlife welfare first. Many marine operators in the Moray Firth are now accredited to a Dolphin Space Programme, while the Scottish Marine Wildlife Operators Association has its own voluntary code of conduct on the West Coast. SNH, the Scottish Executive's environment agency, is developing its own Marine Wildlife Watching Code to fulfil the requirements of the Nature Conservation (Scotland) Act 2004.

Wildlife watchers also have an important individual responsibility. Scotland's most vulnerable species are protected under the Wildlife and Countryside Act 1981. Amendments brought about by the Nature Conservation (Scotland) Act 2004 make it a criminal offence to intentionally or recklessly disturb any birds included in Schedule 1 of the Act whilst on or near the nest, while a licence is also required from SNH to photograph Schedule 1 species at the nest. Animals listed on Schedule 5 of the Act are afforded similar protection. For more information, visit the SNH website (www.snh.org.uk).

Sadly, egg collecting remains a problem and the nest sites of rare species are kept quiet out of necessity. Any suspicious activity should be reported to local police. All forces now have dedicated wildlife crime officers.

When to visit

Scotland has year-round wildlife appeal, although there are peaks in activity through the seasons. Here are some general periods to be aware of:

February to October gannets at colonies

April displaying waders, 'sky dancing' hen harriers

April to May capercaillie and black grouse at the lek

April to late-July osprey at eyries

May corncrake arrive from Africa

May to mid-July majority of seabirds at colonies

May to September increased whale and dolphin activity, plus basking sharks

June common seals pup, red deer calve

June to July machair grassland in full bloom

Late-September to October red deer rut

September to March wintering geese and swans from the north, large flocks of ducks and waders

October to November grey seals pup

Risks and how to avoid them

Some of the destinations in this guide require care, particularly around sea cliffs and when exploring more remote areas. When setting out on longer expeditions, consider your fitness, check regional weather forecasts and pack sensibly. Even in summer, it is recommended to take warm, waterproof clothing, although it is not advisable to wear waterproofs near cliff edges – a slip here could be fatal. For longer trips, take plenty of food and water and leave a route plan with a friend or relative in case of emergency. Midge repellent is also worth carrying.

Access

The Land Reform (Scotland) Act introduced in 2003 provided an official stamp on the 'right to roam', although in many respects it simply reinforced a strong tradition of public access to the countryside for recreational purposes. A key difference, however, is that under the Act the right of access depends on whether it is exercised responsibly.

Similarly, landowners also have an obligation not to unreasonably prevent or deter those seeking access. The responsibilities of the public and land managers are now set out in the Scottish Outdoor Access Code.

However, at certain times of the year there are special restrictions that should be respected. These often concern farming,

shooting and forest activities: if in any doubt, ask. Signs are usually posted at main access points with details. There should be no expectation of a right of access to all places at all times. In addition, the right of access does not extend to use of motor vehicles on private or estate roads.

Seasonal restrictions

Red and sika deer stalking:
Stags: 1 July to 20 October
Hinds: 21 October to 15 February
Deer may be culled at other times for welfare reasons. The seasons for fallow and roe deer (less common) are also longer. Many estates belong to the Hillphones Network which provides advance notice of shoots.
Grouse shooting: 12 August to 10 December
Forestry: Felling: all year
Planting: November to May
Heather burning: September to April
Lambing: March to May (dogs should be kept on a lead at all times near livestock)

A vivid landscape of rolling hills and an often rugged coastline makes much of the area between Scotland's Central Belt and the border with England as enticing as anything found further north – a surprise to many first-time visitors.

This deceptively large region is book ended by two great estuaries: the Firth of Forth in the north and the Solway Firth to the south. Both are important sites for thousands of migrant birds, including the entire Svalbard population of barnacle geese that decamps to the Solway for the winter.

The often spectacular dusk and dawn flights of Southern Scotland's wintering hordes can be experienced at Aberlady Bay – just a stone's throw from Edinburgh – as well as two points on the Solway: Caerlaverock and Mersehead.

In spring, the region's winter visitors are replaced by returning seabirds, the sight, sound and smell of which can be enjoyed

along the impressive cliffs at St Abb's Head and at the Mull of Galloway – Scotland's most southerly point.

This chapter also includes offshore adventures to the seething gannet colonies on Bass Rock and Ailsa Craig before heading inland in search of more elusive creatures: red squirrel and red kite at Ken-Dee Marshes and unsurpassed views of breeding peregrine falcon at the Falls of Clyde.

Southern Scotland

Aberlady Bay Local Nature Reserve

Getting there **25km east of Edinburgh on A198 by Aberlady. Limited parking by footbridge** OS Map Landranger 66

A low-key reserve within striking distance of Edinburgh, Aberlady Bay is one of the most important sites for wintering waders and wildfowl in the Firth of Forth.

Established in 1952, Britain's first Local Nature Reserve runs alongside Gullane's celebrated Number One and Two golf courses roughly halfway between Edinburgh and North Berwick. The reserve's abundant and much studied bird life is attracted by a rich mosaic of habitat including extensive inter-tidal mudflats and pioneer saltmarsh – the latter a rarity in this part of Scotland.

Largely privately owned, but managed by East Lothian Council, the reserve packs much into a small area, including a hidden freshwater loch, woodland, grassland, marsh and extensive dunes.

Also widespread are dense thickets of prickly sea buckthorn. Although originally planted to arrest soil erosion and now providing food and shelter for many birds, sea buckthorn is an invasive species that can quickly colonise more open areas. Each year, volunteer groups take on the sometimes painful work of removing seedlings and digging up outlying clumps.

Significant bird life is present year round at Aberlady Bay. In spring and summer, great care is taken to protect breeding species, including locally important populations of lapwing, redshank, shelduck, reed bunting and various species of warbler.

Summer is also a colourful time at Aberlady Bay with rich botanical interest,

◄ Looking west towards Arthur's Seat in Edinburgh

Shooting submarines

At the head of the beach at low tide can be seen the remains of two XT-craft midget submarines. The craft were towed to Aberlady Bay in 1946, moored to a large concrete block and used for target practice by the RAF. The more southerly of the two is in slightly better condition. Incredibly given their size, each craft was operated by four men.

but is perhaps overshadowed by the sheer variety of bird life that arrives each autumn. From October to April, the reserve supports thousands of passage and wintering wading birds, including priority species such as knot and golden plover, and a significant proportion of the Firth of Forth's wintering wildfowl population.

Numbers of wigeon, eider and shelduck all build up from September, while congregations of long-tailed ducks, scoters (common and velvet) and red-throated divers gather further out and in neighbouring Gullane Bay. Autumn is also an excellent time to spot raptors such as sparrowhawk, kestrel and short-eared owl as they hunt over the reserve.

However, the greatest autumn spectacle comes at dusk when up to 20,000 pink-footed geese return from surrounding farmland to roost on the mudflats – a sight made even more impressive thanks to the backdrop of Arthur's Seat in Edinburgh, the Pentland Hills and the Fife coastline.

Cross the timber bridge over the Peffer Burn and stick to clear paths that run between the golf course and the bay for 4km before dropping onto a large expanse of sandy beach. Allow plenty of time, particularly if investigating the nearby submarine wrecks or continuing round to Gullane Point. Visitors at dawn or dusk might catch sight of the reserve's small herd of roe deer.

The colourful shelduck feeds on shellfish and invertebrates

Bass Rock

Getting there **Boat trips from North Berwick harbour, 40km east of Edinburgh**
OS Map **Landranger 66**

Sugar-coated by more than 100,000 gannets, Bass Rock offers one of the most arresting wildlife spectacles in Scotland.

Just 5km off the mainland, Bass Rock is an iconic landmark on the East Lothian coastline. Originally the plug of an old volcano, it is famous for the thousands of gannets that return to the same mate and nest site each year (Jan-Oct).

Seen from ashore when the birds are in residence, Bass Rock appears a place of serene beauty. Up close, however, it could not be more different as the inhabitants of the world's largest single rock gannet colony conduct their daily battle for space, food and survival.

The birds were once harvested for their feathers, fat and for food, but are now protected. Today, the gannets of Bass Rock are in good health, with the population increasing by some 5 per cent per annum. Year-on-year growth was, until recently, produced from the colony's own output, but has now been bolstered by immigration from elsewhere.

Gannets occupy a key feeding niche amongst seabirds in Scotland: their ability to forage further and deeper for a wide variety of prey means that gannets have been largely unaffected by the poor breeding success that has blighted so many other species in recent years.

Gannet pairs form a real bond and exhibit complex behaviour as they work together to defend nest sites and ward off gulls scouting for unprotected eggs. While devoted to each other, each pair endures

◀ Bass Rock from the shore

a stormy relationship with its neighbours; quarrels are common, particularly when birds blunder into land too close to another pair's nest site.

Unusually for seabirds, gannets linger late into the year, with the last chicks heading out to sea in October. Many travel as far as the West African coast and will not return for several years until ready to breed. Adult and immature birds, meanwhile, spend the winter fishing mainly off European coasts.

But while gannets undoubtedly dominate, the lower ledges of the sheer cliffs also house shag, guillemot and various gulls,

plus a few razorbill and kittiwake in the less accessible areas. The ruins of the old fortifications around the landing area also hold a handful of nesting puffin.

Boat trips around Bass Rock run from North Berwick harbour, although landing can only be arranged via the nearby Scottish Seabird Centre. While on the water, look out for bottlenose dolphins that are sometimes seen close inshore, as well as plunge-diving gannets on the final approach.

For those able to land, the resident gulls ensure that any walk along the path from the lighthouse up to the ruins of a 15th-century chapel is a raucous experience. The views back to Tantallon Castle and further down the East Lothian coast are worth the trip alone.

High-tech wildlife viewing

The Scottish Seabird Centre is one of the country's most successful wildlife visitor centres with more than a million people having passed through its doors since opening in 2000. The centre offers a year-round wildlife experience and has developed an expertise in remote viewing. With webcams trained on Bass Rock and the nearby island of Fidra, visitors can enjoy intimate views of seabirds in the summer, plus grey seal pups on the Isle of May between October and December.

Gannets nest in tightly packed colonies

St Abb's Head National Trust for Scotland

Getting there Park at Northfield Farm, 3km north of Coldingham. Interpretive centre (open April-Oct) **OS Map** Landranger 67

Tucked away on the Berwickshire coast, St Abb's Head holds a large seabird colony and is part of the country's first voluntary marine reserve.

From May to mid-July this NTS-managed section of coastline is home to one of mainland Scotland's most impressive seabird colonies, including kittiwake, guillemot, razorbill, shag and fulmar. The hard volcanic cliffs also support a handful of puffin. Some 60,000 seabirds breed at the head itself, although there are also discrete colonies up and down the coast.

In early July, and before they can fly, razorbill and guillemot chicks plunge from their precarious ledges into the water below. This impressive leap of faith usually takes place during the hours of darkness to avoid predators, after which the fledglings are taken out to sea by their parents to learn the art of fishing and survival.

During spring and summer, a carpet of hardy plants provides a rolling mosaic of colour along the clifftops and surrounding coastal heath. Flowers such as sea campion, purple milk vetch and rock rose in turn

Cliff hanging

Visitors can now enjoy guided trips along the previously inaccessible clifftops north of St Abb's Head thanks to an innovative agreement struck between local landowners. Led by a trained biologist and local expert, Clifftop Discovery provides an adventurous journey along the cliffs by Land Rover. Emphasis is placed on the area's geological, archaeological and botanical importance, as well as its wildlife. Trips run from March and extend into November to include the pupping of grey seals in sheltered coves along the coast.

Kittiwake on the nest

attract butterflies ranging from meadow browns and common blues to the rare northern brown argus.

And while the seabirds and flora lure visitors to the cliffs, the abundant marine life in the clear waters below makes the area popular with scuba divers and sea kayakers. A mixture of currents ensures that Atlantic and Arctic species – the latter at the edge of their southerly range – are found here.

Since 1984, the waters around the Head have been part of the St Abbs and Eyemouth Voluntary Marine Reserve – the first of its kind in Scotland. Today, conservation bodies, recreational users and the local commercial fishing industry continue their collaborative effort to protect the area's marine life.

From Northfield Farm, a circular walk (4.8km) runs along the clifftops and returns via the lighthouse access road. Although there is plenty of action along the way, the best views can be found in the open bowl around Nunnery Point, just northwest of the lighthouse.

With care, it is possible to get close to some of the heavily populated outlying stacks. This is a good area to scan for the few puffins that nest in the area, while squadrons of gannets can be seen flying past on their way to and from the nearby colony at Bass Rock. NTS rangers also offer guided walks throughout the summer.

◄ Busy seabird ledges around Nunnery Point

Falls of Clyde Scottish Wildlife Trust

Getting there New Lanark village, off A73. SWT visitor centre (open year round, check seasonal hours) at Old Mill Dyeworks. Admission charge OS Map Landranger 72

Breeding peregrine falcons share a historic gorge with badgers and bats – all within touching distance of a popular World Heritage Site.

Formed by retreating glaciers and shaped by the tumbling River Clyde, the sandstone gorge that runs through the Falls of Clyde Wildlife Reserve has played its part in the gradual recovery of the peregrine falcon in Scotland.

Although not evenly distributed, peregrine numbers have begun to rebound from the dark days of the 1950s – a time when widespread use of agricultural pesticides contaminated prey items to such an extent that many peregrines were left infertile.

Today, two-thirds of the UK's 1500 breeding pairs nest in Scotland, although the threat of egg theft as well as illegal persecution (shooting and poisoning) still casts a lengthy shadow.

Peregrines first nested at the Falls of Clyde in 1997 and have bred on the ledges along the gorge ever since. During this time, more than 20 chicks have successfully fledged – thanks in no small part to round-the-clock monitoring by SWT staff and volunteers. A 24-hour vigil is maintained from when the birds first occupy the nest in early April to when the chicks fledge in July.

A screened approach and powerful telescopes allow outstanding views of the nest without causing disturbance. With luck, the adults can sometimes be seen returning with food – either freshly dispatched or retrieved from a hidden larder ledge where previous kills are stored.

Peregrines feed almost exclusively on other birds, stooping at tremendous speed to take prey in midair. Their diet consists mainly of songbirds although a taste for

◄ A frosty Mill Weir deep in the gorge

Seeking inspiration

The three main falls, or linns in Scots – Bonnington, Corra and Stonebyres – and the heavily wooded gorge they occupy have attracted visitors for centuries, including celebrated artists and writers. The gorge is also of great historical interest with a ruined castle, an 18th-century pavilion and a power station that has harnessed the energy of the Bonnington and Corra waterfalls since 1927. And then there is New Lanark itself – a restored 18th-century cotton mill village now celebrated as a World Heritage Site.

pigeons can cause disquiet among fanciers. Formidable hunters, these crow-sized falcons have even been known to tackle birds as large as a heron.

Once fledged, the juveniles stay with their parents for up to three months, but are chased away in autumn to reduce competition for food. The adults remain in the area throughout the year, but are difficult to see outside the breeding season.

Elsewhere, the mixed woodland in the gorge is home to several active badger setts as well as five species of bat.

These include a colony of Daubenton's – a river bat – that roosts in the ruins of the 15th-century Corra Castle on the west side of the gorge. SWT staff run badger watching evenings and bat walks from May to September.

The recently renovated SWT visitor centre provides a good starting point for exploring the area: it offers CCTV links to the peregrine nest, plus highlights from previous badger watching evenings. From here, walk 1.6km along an attractive riverside trail to reach the nest, looking out for roe deer, dippers and kingfishers on the way.

Peregrine falcon with young

Caerlaverock Wildfowl and Wetlands Trust

Getting there 14km southeast of Dumfries off the B725 Glencaple road. Visitor centre (open year round). Admission charge
OS Map Landranger 84

Wintering barnacle geese and whooper swans head the cast at this well-equipped wildlife viewing centre.

Caerlaverock is one of nine Wildfowl and Wetlands Trust (WWT) reserves in the UK, although the only one in Scotland. True to a philosophy of making wildlife as accessible as possible, Caerlaverock's network of towers, hides, screened approaches and seasonal trails allow guaranteed close up views of an array of wildfowl and waders throughout the year.

The centre's latest facility, the Saltcot Merse Observatory, provides excellent views back over the reserve and across the Solway Firth. This is an ideal spot from which to watch thousands of waders and shorebirds pushed up at high tide, as well as hen harrier, peregrine falcon and short-eared owl working the saltmarsh (or merse).

WWT founder Sir Peter Scott established Caerlaverock in 1970 specifically to provide a safe home for the Svalbard population of barnacle geese that winter on the Solway between September and late April. These maritime, grass-feeding birds are attracted by the area's relatively benign winters, safe roost sites on the mudflats and merse, and abundance of good grazing on nearby coastal fields. Some of the geese make the 3200km journey in just 48 hours.

Barnacle numbers have increased dramatically since the 1940s when the Svalbard population was hit by shooting, severe Arctic weather and the use of their Solway wintering grounds for military

◄ The Saltcot Merse Observatory

Bears and barnacles

While barnacle goose numbers at Caerlaverock have generally increased, there is concern about a recent decline in the number of goslings – with the finger being pointed at climate change and its impact on polar bear behaviour in the high Arctic. Retreating sea ice has prevented Svalbard's polar bears from reaching favoured prey, such as seals, forcing them ashore much earlier in the barnacle breeding season than usual. Some have turned to eggs and goslings to make up the shortfall, with one female and her cub seen to work through almost 900 nests in a recent season.

activities. Subsequent work between the WWT, the local farming community and other bodies has seen the Svalbard population increase from just 300 birds in the late 1940s to around 26,000 today.

In addition, Caerlaverock is also the winter home to around 500 whooper swans that arrive from Iceland each autumn. The adult whoopers and their cygnets join other opportunistic wildfowl to feast on grain served up twice-daily by wardens (11am and 2pm). Watching the melee from inside a large, glass-fronted

observatory is about as close as it is possible to get to wild whooper swans.

Come spring, the geese and swans return north, their yapping and honking making way for the sound of migrating songbirds and the call of rare natterjack toads.

The centre offers guided walks and out-of-hours events throughout the year, including geese flighting at sunrise, evening badger watches and the spawning of natterjack toads under cover of darkness. Self-catering farmhouse accommodation is available onsite.

Whooper swans gather at feeding time

17

Mersehead RSPB Reserve

Getting there **24km southwest of Dumfries, signposted from A710 at Caulkerbush. Visitor centre (open year round), hides and trails** OS Map **Landranger 84**

Noisy flocks of barnacle geese in winter and a successful breeding wader programme in spring make Mersehead one of the Solway's most prized wildlife sites.

Enviably situated between rolling hills and the north shore of the inner Solway, the RSPB reserve at Mersehead is best known for the thousands of barnacle geese that arrive from their Svalbard breeding grounds in late September.

Around 10,000 barnacles – or 30 per cent of the Svalbard population – use the reserve's mudflats and neighbouring fields to roost and feed, although their excited yapping suggests even greater numbers. Despite being naturally wary, the flocks can be enjoyed at extremely close quarters, particularly in the fields around the visitor centre.

But as impressive as they are, there is much more to Mersehead than just wintering geese. Once a mixed farm, the RSPB purchased the site in 1993 and has since undertaken conservation work across a wide variety of habitat that includes wetland, grazed grassland, wild bird cover crops, inter-tidal mudflats and merse.

And each section of the reserve now attracts specific wildlife. In winter, the cereal crops are a magnet for flocks of farmland birds, which in turn lure raptors such as peregrine and hen harrier. Elsewhere, the flooding of already wet meadows provides shelter for large numbers of ducks, including

Barnacle geese are wary feeders

wigeon, teal, shoveler and pintail.

Out on the Solway mudflats, many thousands of passage and wintering waders bank and wheel as they follow the tide, with particularly large numbers of oystercatcher, curlew and dunlin. Further out still, a collection of divers, grebes and scoters can sometimes be seen swimming close to shore at high tide.

In spring, controlled flooding and livestock grazing has helped create ideal conditions for breeding waders – a combination of marshy ground (for feeding) and drier areas (for nesting). From a very low base, numbers of lapwing, snipe and redshank – the three core species targeted – have greatly increased, while oystercatcher and curlew have also benefited.

In addition to its bird life, the Solway merse – the largest expanse of such habitat in Scotland – also supports rarities such as a breeding colony of natterjack toads. The entire Scottish population is found along this coastline, their steady croaking a feature of still evenings in April and May.

Two hides overlook the meadows and can be excellent spots to spy otters hunting over the wetlands. Both are accessed from the visitor centre as part of either a 3km wetland trail or a 4km coastal trail. The latter offers striking views across the Solway to the Lake District in England.

Displaying lapwing

A familiar farmland bird, the lapwing has been one of the chief beneficiaries of ongoing breeding wader efforts at Mersehead. Highly vocal and with a distinctive head crest, the birds can be seen displaying manically over parts of the reserve in spring. Although the species has suffered serious decline across the UK in recent years, numbers at Mersehead have jumped from just two breeding pairs in 1993 to more than 70 today.

◀ Looking south across the Solway mudflats

Ken-Dee Marshes RSPB Reserve

Getting there Car park at Mains of Duchrae Farm on minor road north from Glenlochar to A762. Hides and trail
OS Map Landranger 84

A walk through the mixed woodland along the western shore of Loch Ken provides good opportunities to spot many local specialties.

Created by the damming of the River Dee at Glenlochar for a hydroelectric scheme in the 1930s, Loch Ken has become a popular destination for watersports, angling, and increasingly, wildlife watching.

The RSPB manages several pockets of land nearby, although the most interesting mix of habitat and species is found at this small reserve along the loch's quieter western shore. Here, in an area of particular significance for breeding and wintering birds, the RSPB has isolated a section of loch to create a marshy lagoon where water levels can be readily controlled.

Although Ken-Dee Marshes has year-round appeal – including breeding waders, ducks and woodland birds in summer – late autumn and winter are often the best times to visit. From November, the low-lying fields and wet grassland attract several hundred rare Greenland white-fronted geese, which mingle with larger numbers of wintering greylags and pink-footed geese.

Greenland white-fronts have a distinctive white patch between the beak and the front of the head, as well as dark bars across the belly. There is a goose-viewing platform just off the main (2.4km) trail that leads through the reserve from the car park.

In addition to the geese, there are fine views along Loch Ken, while visitors should also keep an eye out for the red kites that

◀ One of two hides overlooking Ken-Dee's man-made lagoon

Galloway Kite Trail

A major nature-based tourism initiative in the area, this circular drive around Loch Ken highlights the growing local population of red kites following the bird's reintroduction in 2001. The drive includes several information boards and viewpoints that can be explored on foot, as well as a feeding station at Bellymack Hill Farm near Laurieston. One of two such stations in Scotland – the other near Stirling (see p46) – the site attracts up to 30 birds at a time and is particularly lively in winter. Food is put out for the birds each day at 2pm.

frequent the area following reintroduction in Galloway in 2001.

The main trail continues past open fields and through deciduous woodland on its way to two hides: both with views across a wetland landscape frequented by heron, various ducks – such as teal, wigeon and pintail – and even the occasional otter.

Meanwhile, woodland residents such as great spotted woodpecker and red squirrel also make full use of the nut feeders in front of the hides – the latter a frequent sight at Ken-Dee and with something of a stronghold in Dumfries and Galloway generally.

Although able to live in most kinds of woodland, Scotland's native red squirrels are now generally restricted to conifer plantations and native pinewoods. One problem in deciduous woodland is that reds do not have the same flexibility of diet as the North American greys that

continue to expand territory in Scotland.

Greys, for instance, can feed on hazelnuts at an earlier stage and are also able to fully digest and gain maximum nutrition from other sources, such as acorns.

Red squirrels can be seen here at any time, although early in the year when the animals are courting – and therefore less wary – can be a particularly good time.

A feasting red squirrel

Mull of Galloway RSPB Reserve

Getting there **8km south of Drummore off A716. Signposted along minor roads. Visitor centre (open Easter to mid-Oct)** OS Map **Landranger 82**

Worth the trip for the scenery alone, Scotland's most southerly point is home to a small but busy seabird colony and abundant marine life.

Although off the beaten track, the Mull of Galloway nonetheless attracts a steady flow of visitors each year, drawn by dazzling Solway views and the wildlife that inhabits the precipitous cliffs at the southern tip of Scotland.

This small RSPB reserve is at its most lively in spring and early summer; the maritime heath and cliff tops are painted in an array of colours, attracting a variety of butterflies and birds, while on the cliffs themselves the reserve's seabird colony is in full cry.

Although modest by Scottish standards, the 7,000 seabirds that pack the headland make this the largest mainland colony in southwest Scotland. The 85m-high cliffs hold good numbers of fulmar, guillemot, razorbill, kittiwake and shag, with great views of the nesting birds, particularly around the now disused foghorn.

More elusive are the small numbers of black guillemot (or tysties) that nest beneath boulders and in rock crevices near the base of the cliffs. They are joined by a small number of puffins, a species that normally nests in burrows but has to be flexible at mainland sites where foxes and rats pose a threat to eggs and chicks.

Fulmar pair at the nest

Keep your distance

The cackling of fulmars at the nest is a familiar sound on seabird cliffs, but the birds should be approached with caution. This far-foraging cousin of the albatross is unique in that it is able to convert food to lipids (oil) in its large stomach. Although the oil is used primarily as a source of energy for long fishing trips at sea, it also has another purpose: when threatened, fulmars can project an alarmingly accurate stream of this foul-smelling substance up to a distance of two metres. While unpleasant for humans, fulmar stomach oil can be deadly for other birds as it destroys their vital waterproofing.

While the puffins are unmistakeable with their brightly coloured beaks in summer, black guillemots have some striking features of their own: black with white wing patches, the birds' feet and gape are coloured a deep red – the latter obvious when it makes its high-pitched whistling call.

Both puffin and black guillemot are best spotted rafting on the surface of the water – although the latter can be seen at much closer quarters at Portpatrick (12km south of Stranraer) where small numbers nest in the harbour wall (April to July).

Back at the Mull, summer sees an almost constant stream of gannets passing the headland on their way to and from a colony at Scare Rocks, 10km off the coast. Also keep an eye on the waters below – grey seals and harbour porpoise are frequently seen, while basking sharks occasionally drift past on calm days.

An RSPB warden mans a visitor centre near the lighthouse during the summer, which includes CCTV cameras that can zoom in on particularly active parts of the cliff. The lighthouse itself is open to the public at weekends (April-Sept), while nearby is one of the most dramatically located coffee houses in Scotland with views to the Isle of Man and Ireland's Antrim Hills.

◀ Grand views over the Solway

Ailsa Craig RSPB Reserve

Getting there 16km off South Ayrshire coast. Daily sailings from Girvan during summer OS Map Landranger 76

Nicknamed 'Paddy's Milestone' for its location halfway between Glasgow and Belfast, Ailsa Craig holds a major gannetry and a growing number of other seabirds.

Climbing to a height of 340m and with sheer cliffs on three sides, the formidable Ailsa Craig looms on the horizon west of Girvan. A source of high-quality granite used for producing curling stones, it was once home to a handful of quarry workers as well as lighthouse operators before automation.

Now uninhabited, but populated by upwards of 40,000 pairs of gannet – only St Kilda and Bass Rock hold more in the UK – the island was recently leased to the RSPB to manage as a nature reserve.

Unusually for seabirds, gannets spend most of their time ashore: the birds arrive in late January and linger until October, often several weeks after chicks have fledged. Such early arrival and late departure is closely linked with the need to defend hard-won nest sites that are often retained for life.

In amongst the growing gannet colony are other cliff-nesting seabirds, including guillemot, razorbill, kittiwake and fulmar, while the interior holds less familiar species such as a thriving population of slow worms.

And the hope is that Ailsa Craig will gradually become more diverse still with the return of some long-lost breeding species. Once a west coast stronghold for puffin, the population was decimated following the arrival of brown rats that landed as stowaways.

However, some 10 years after an eradication project led by the University of Glasgow, Ailsa Craig is once again rat-free and puffins have begun to return. The birds bred here in 2000 for the first time in 50 years and numbers continue to increase each season.

◀ Ailsa Craig from Girvan beach

Other species vulnerable to rat predation have also shown signs of recovery: the boulder beach below the cliffs now holds around 100 pairs of shag and a handful of breeding black guillemot. Manx shearwaters – a burrow-nester like the puffin – have also been seen and heard over the island at night during the breeding season, although it is not yet clear whether they are actively prospecting for nest sites.

Although it appears tantalisingly close, Ailsa Craig can be difficult to access: the island is isolated and the weather in the Firth of Clyde can turn quickly. Private operators run boat trips from Girvan, although only one (*MFV Glorious*) is licensed to land.

The island has a single path to the highest point, but the going is tough over steep terrain. While the views are magnificent, the birds that cling to the overhanging cliffs are much better experienced from the sea.

Precision diving

In addition to the sound of so many gannets packed into a small area, one of the highlights of a boat trip around Ailsa Craig is watching these goose-sized birds plunge dive for shoaling fish, often from a great height. Equipped with binocular vision, gannets are able to target prey such as herring and mackerel near the surface with great precision. They are also built to withstand the tremendous impact when entering the water: a protective membrane covers the eyes, while a layer of air cells beneath the skin cushions its torpedo-shaped head.

25

The various sea cliffs, sand spits and dune systems that are such a feature of Scotland's east coast as it stretches north from Fife include several outstanding wildlife watching sites – often holding particularly large gatherings of some of the country's finest species.

Although offshore, the tone is set by the most striking of the Firth of Forth's small islands: the Isle of May. An excellent place to see puffins, usually at close quarters, the island is also home to a large colony of breeding grey seals. Outside the breeding season, many of the animals also spend time on the wispy sandbanks at Tentsmuir Point where they are joined by hundreds of common seals.

This theme of large gatherings of particular species continues along the coast with huge numbers of wintering pink-footed geese at Montrose Basin, a wonderful seabird colony at Fowlsheugh and thousands of breeding eider ducks behind the dunes at Forvie.

This chapter also includes two inland sites, each with a very different character: Loch of Kinnordy is a tranquil spot for enjoying a variety of bird life, while Corrie Fee provides an atmospheric gateway to an upland area inhabited by golden eagle, mountain hare and ptarmigan.

26

Angus and the East Coast

Isle of May Scottish Natural Heritage

Getting there **Sailings from Anstruther on the *May Princess* (May-Sept). Boats also operate from North Berwick** OS Map **Landranger 59**

Thousands of seabirds, a major seal colony and a colourful history make this one of the most alluring islands in the Firth of Forth.

Chugging up the narrow sea channel to the main landing area at Kirkhaven provides a taste of what is to come: whirling seabirds, the chatter of terns and plenty of grey seals.

A National Nature Reserve since 1956, and now owned by SNH, the Isle of May guards the outer Firth of Forth some 8km off the coast of Fife. At the height of a strong breeding season, this small island (1.5km by 0.5km) teems with upwards of 200,000 breeding seabirds. A total of 13 species breed here including significant numbers of eider duck – often nesting close to footpaths – kittiwake, guillemot, razorbill and Arctic tern.

The island is also home to the single largest puffin colony in Britain (around 68,000 pairs) and the birds can be seen rafting on the sea or sitting in tight groups almost anywhere between late April and mid-July.

This huge colony of seabirds has been subject to detailed scientific research since the 1930s, mainly by the Centre for Ecology and Hydrology, while SNH now has a full-time presence on the island between April and October. Rangers and volunteers divide their time between monitoring the number and productivity of each species

Puffin in full cry

and meeting visitors to the island.

Although the seabirds here have not suffered from the same food shortages as colonies elsewhere in Scotland, the waters of the Firth of Forth are no longer as rich as they once were. Variations in the marine ecosystem, with climate change considered the chief culprit, have seen a redistribution of the plant and animal plankton that props up the food chain – with seabird breeding success now mixed as a result.

The island is also home to the largest colony of grey seals on the east coast of Scotland and the animals can be seen hauled up at low tide at either end of the island or swimming beneath the west cliffs all year round.

However, their numbers swell to some 5000 individuals between September and December when mothers come ashore and give birth to almost 2000 pups. Visits by the public are not possible during this time, but this remarkable spectacle can be viewed from the remote cameras installed at the Scottish Seabird Centre in North Berwick.

Rangers meet all landing parties and point visitors towards a series of roped-off paths that criss-cross the island. Stick to the walkways as even a slight deviation could crush puffin burrows or disturb female eiders on the nest. Up to three hours are spent ashore depending on tide and weather conditions.

War and worship

Over the centuries, man has used the Isle of May for a mixture of war and worship with the first people thought to have visited around 4000 years ago. The island has since served as a haven for religious retreat and was the site of Scotland's first manned light beacon (in 1636). During World War One, the island was home to a signal station built to warn of enemy vessels in the Firth of Forth. The Admiralty occupied it again in the 1930s when the island's main role was to locate and identify all ships entering the Forth.

◀ Above the main landing area at Kirkhaven

Tentsmuir Point Scottish Natural Heritage

Getting there 2.5km north of Forestry Commission car park at Kinshaldy off B945, or 4km east of Tayport (limited parking) OS Map Landranger 59

An expanse of dunes and sandbars on the Tay estuary that holds thousands of wintering eider ducks and an impressive year-round seal population.

Dominated by grassy sand dunes, Tentsmuir Point is an incredibly fragile landmass that changes shape almost on a daily basis. The reserve's shifting sands extend up to five metres per year at its most northerly point, while the sea consumes a roughly equal area of beach further south.

The sheer scale – and speed – of this coastal realignment is best illustrated by a line of concrete anti-tank blocks erected in 1941 at what was once the high tide line.

Much of the new land comes from sand blown in from Abertay Sands, a wispy system of sandbanks that stretch eastwards for several kilometres at low tide. These intricate formations are created by sediment deposited as the powerful River Tay meets the swirling currents of the North Sea.

The Tay is a hugely important site for wildfowl, waders and other shorebirds, particularly between October and March. Thousands of pink-footed geese use the sandbanks and foreshore for roosting, while bar-tailed godwit, grey plover and many other species feed along the margins of sand and sea.

Meanwhile, in the outer Tay, thousands of eider ducks – the UK's largest winter gathering – feast on the abundant mussels that grow on the gravel seabed.

Tentsmuir Point is also known for its year-round population of seals – both grey and common. As many as 1600 greys regularly haul out on Abertay Sands, while several hundred commons also use the sandbars. Few seem bothered by the periodic

Grey seal pup

Survival of the fattest

Grey seal pups must grow up fast if they are to survive: they are weaned for up to 31 days and then abandoned by their mothers. The high fat content of the mothers' milk provides vital reserves of energy, stored as blubber. Most pups remain on the birthing beaches for several weeks living off this fat supply before eventually venturing, often famished, into the water. Pups head out to sea completely unprepared, often learning hunting skills from older seals. Not surprisingly, early mortality rates are high, particularly amongst males, while up to 40 per cent of pups do not survive the first year.

manoeuvres from nearby RAF Leuchars.

Common seals breed on the sandbanks in the summer, whereas the larger greys prefer more isolated spots such as the Isle of May where they breed later in the year (Sept-Dec), although they also occasionally pup on the foreshore.

Summer visitors to the reserve may notice Highland cattle grazing the dunes between the foreshore and the planted forest behind; the animals are used as part of a programme of tree and scrub removal designed to protect this pristine, but vulnerable, dune habitat.

During this time, the waterlogged soil between dune ridges provides perfect conditions for plants such as ragged robin, northern marsh orchid and bird's foot trefoil to flourish – in turn attracting many species of butterfly and moth.

From the car park at Kinshaldy, head north along the forest track or foreshore to the sandbanks. Watch for lines of loafing seals at low tide and plenty of bobbing heads at other times. Alternatively, park in Tayport and walk in along the foreshore, looking out for the many birds that use the mudflats and scalps.

◀ Grey seals haul out on the many sandbars around Tentsmuir Point

Loch of Kinnordy RSPB Reserve

Getting there 1.6km west of Kirriemuir on B951. Also linked by footpath from Kirriemuir. Hides and trail. Open daily (9.00am–dusk) OS Map Landranger 54

Nestled in the shadow of the Angus Braes, Loch of Kinnordy provides a small but important haven for many breeding and wintering birds.

Set in a low-lying basin surrounded by farmland, Loch of Kinnordy once covered a much larger area. In the 1800s, the loch was drained and quarried for its underlying marl – a type of clay used as fertiliser – before being levelled and later reverting to the current mix of mire, marsh and open water.

Today, this shallow loch attracts a variety of bird life throughout the year, although for the time being it has lost some of its star turns. Kinnordy was once home to a substantial colony of black-headed gulls (roughly 8000 pairs), but the colony has experienced heavy decline in recent years.

One possible cause is a gradual change in vegetation: the gulls had previously nested on dense mats of bogbean, but gradual silting of the loch precipitated the growth of branched bur-reed beneath where the colony used to gather. And as the colony reduced in size, it became less able to ward off predators – so speeding its further decline.

Today, only around 30 pairs of black-headed gulls attempt to nest, although the RSPB hopes that by reducing vegetation levels elsewhere and reversing the silting of the loch, this rather transient species will

Skulking snipe

Often seen on fenceposts or exploding from thick cover, snipe are best known for their aerial drumming display in spring and early summer – a bizarre throbbing sound created by air vibrating through outstretched tail feathers. These skulking waders have very specific needs when it comes to breeding habitat: tall vegetation, a high water table (for protection) and wet areas with soft soil that can be easily probed for earthworms and insect larvae. The wet grassland being created at Loch of Kinnordy is ideal.

one day return in greater numbers.

The loss of such a large gull colony has also affected another Kinnordy speciality: the black-necked grebe. Up to 11 pairs of this rare breeding bird – essentially the entire UK population – used to nest within the gull colony for protection, but has now moved elsewhere.

However, Kinnordy still attracts important numbers of summer and wintering species. The local osprey population are regular users of the loch, often fishing here for pike and perch several times a day in the summer.

The loch also holds many species of breeding duck, as well as a growing number of waders, including lapwing, snipe and redshank. All have benefited from the

removal of willow scrub from the marsh, seasonal adjustment of water levels and the grazing of Highland cattle to create larger areas of suitable habitat around the loch edges.

From September, the first whooper swans and pink-footed geese begin to arrive from their northern breeding grounds, while goldeneye, goosander and teal numbers also build up. Being shallow, Kinnordy freezes easily – an especially good time to spot the resident otters as they skitter across the ice to reach open water.

As with much of the wildlife here, they are often best seen from the seclusion of one of three hides, all easily reached from the reserve car park.

◀ *Loch of Kinnordy seen from the roadside*

Corrie Fee Scottish Natural Heritage

Getting there **Accessed from Forestry Commission's Glen Doll car park at head of Glen Clova, off B955 from Kirriemuir**
OS Map **Landranger 44**

Corrie Fee's glacial bowl shelters rare montane flora, while the slopes above harbour classic upland species such as ptarmigan and mountain hare.

A popular winter climbing venue, the enclosed Corrie Fee is one of the most striking glacial features in Glen Clova. For botanists, however, the steep-sided walls are better known for containing some of the finest arctic-alpine flora and montane scrub in Scotland.

Nationally scarce plants such as purple coltsfoot and yellow oxytropis survive on ledges inaccessible to grazing deer, while patches of downy and woolly willow cling doggedly to surrounding crags. And it is the protection and restoration of this upland flora that is central to SNH's management of the reserve — not easy in an area with one of the highest densities of red deer in Scotland.

Heavy grazing over the last 200 years has removed the cover of shrubby juniper, rowan and willow that once carpeted the corrie floor, leaving behind a bare landscape of cropped heather and glacial moraine.

To give regenerating scrub a chance, SNH is working with the Deer Commission for Scotland and local estates to drastically reduce deer numbers. However, reaching what is a much lower target density of animals continues to prove difficult, despite recent increases in culling.

A fenced off area of much of the reserve's scrub willow in the adjacent Corrie Sharroch

Hardy hares

Mountain hares moult into their predominantly white winter coats in late autumn. With warm underfur and an ability to survive on relatively poor-quality food the animals are well suited to coping with harsh upland conditions. Normally a solitary animal, hares sometimes gather in large groups to feed or shelter in shallow scrapes when there is good snow cover. Unlike deer, which tend to traverse slopes, hare runs usually head straight up hill, making it harder for predators such as golden eagle to follow them. An ability to run at speeds of up to 60km per hour can come in just as handy.

highlights what can be achieved when grazing pressure is reduced, although the ultimate goal is to create conditions in which the scrub can regenerate without the need for fencing.

An additional conservation effort focuses on the habitat around the Fee Burn as it meanders along the corrie floor. Although ideal for water vole, one of the UK's most endangered species, predation by mink has taken its toll on the population around the burn. Meanwhile, the small number of voles outside the reserve are unlikely to recolonise until mink have been eradicated – a process that continues together with the Forestry Commission.

Corrie Fee is reached along a 3.5km forest track that rises gradually from the car park at Glen Doll. Look out for red squirrel, siskin and crossbill on the way up and scan the skyline around the corrie itself: peregrine falcon and raven are both present, while golden eagle also hunt in the area.

A newly upgraded path continues up the back of the corrie wall to access the high tops – a strenuous route that requires care in winter. The vast surrounding plateau, much of it above 800m, is home to many upland species: dotterel breed here in the summer, while mountain hare and ptarmigan can be spotted year round, particularly below the broken scree summit of nearby Mayar (928m).

Montrose Basin Scottish Wildlife Trust

Getting there **SWT visitor centre (open year round, check seasonal hours) off A92, 2km south of Montrose. Admission charge**
OS Map **Landranger 54**

A large tidal basin that attracts more than 50,000 wintering wildfowl and waders, including significant numbers of pink-footed geese.

Estuaries are not always known for their scenic beauty, but with dramatic sunsets and a backdrop of the often snow-covered Grampians to the west, Montrose Basin is a definite exception.

Here, a combination of the River South Esk emptying into the enclosed basin and a strong tidal flow makes for a complex estuarine ecosystem. While much of the reserve lies beneath the high water mark, the western end also features elevated areas of saltmarsh, reed swamp and arable land.

Otters are sometimes spotted along the riverbanks and common seals haul out on the mudflats towards Montrose, but the reserve is known mainly for its exceptional bird life. Almost 200 species have been recorded here, with the Basin recognised as one of the most important sites for wildfowl and waders in Scotland.

And the attraction is clear: the Basin offers a largely unpolluted and food-rich environment with many thousands of invertebrates – such as hydrobia (a mud snail) – in every square metre of mud. Other abundant species such as lugworm are equally important ecologically as their feeding and cast production helps re-oxygenate the mud.

Skein of geese

Unlikely bedfellows

Montrose Basin is split almost equally into a sanctuary zone and a wildfowling area – a seemingly unholy alliance between conservationists and hunters. However, the two sides first came together for mutual benefit in the 1960s after uncontrolled shooting saw goose numbers plummet and the future of wildfowling in the Basin threatened. Wildfowling is now much more structured with a permit system and strict species designation contributing to a recovery in goose and duck numbers. Around 1000 birds are still shot in the Basin each winter, although this is not thought to negatively impact the wider population.

Large numbers of pink-footed geese, shelduck, wigeon, knot and redshank all rely on the wide expanse of tidal flats for feeding or roosting. While the majority are winter visitors (Sept-April) or passage migrants (April-May and July-Oct), the reserve also holds more than 50 breeding species, with eider duck the most important.

Although thought to be a non-breeder, osprey also hunt regularly over the Basin in summer and can sometimes be seen out on the mudflats devouring their catch.

However, from September it is the wintering pink-footed geese that offer the greatest spectacle. Much anticipated each year, the first birds usually arrive during the second week in September, with numbers peaking at around 35,000 in November.

Like all pink-foots wintering in Britain, the geese come from the Iceland and Eastern Greenland breeding populations.

These dainty and vocal birds feed on neighbouring farms by day and return to roost on the safety of the mudflats at dusk. The main roost site is at the eastern end of the Basin, although the geese often flock in its northeast corner just before flight each morning, allowing excellent views.

The Scottish Wildlife Trust manages the reserve and its flagship visitor centre is a good first port of call, offering panoramic views, directions to the reserve's three hides, access details and interpretation. Fine views can also be had from the railway bridge at Montrose station, particularly at sundown when skeins of geese come in to roost.

◀ Sunset over Montrose Basin

Fowlsheugh RSPB Reserve

Getting there 5km south of Stonehaven off A92, signposted Crawton. Small car park OS Map Landranger 45

Unmarked and unheralded, Fowlsheugh nonetheless offers close quarter views of one of Scotland's largest mainland seabird colonies.

A single-track road that winds down to a scattering of houses on the coast promises little, but leads to a hidden gem: the sound and smell of upwards of 130,000 breeding seabirds packed tightly against Fowlsheugh's 65m-high sandstone cliffs.

Unlike some colonies, the birds are easily viewed thanks to the reserve's deeply indented cliffs. With care, it is possible to enjoy close-up views without causing disturbance. From April until mid-July, the birds nest in heaving layers with shags and eider ducks braving the sea spray at the base of the cliffs and a small number of puffins in the grassy banks at the top.

In between are kittiwakes (up to 20,000 pairs), one of Scotland's strongest razorbill colonies (6,500 individuals) and tightly packed groups of noisy guillemots (65,000 individuals). Around three per cent of guillemots at Fowlsheugh are bridled, with a distinctive white ring around the eye and a stripe behind it – a genetic quirk increasingly common further north.

Interestingly, Fowlsheugh is one of the few North Sea colonies to have posted consistent breeding success in recent years, albeit with several species doing so later than usual. Such productivity could be attributed to local factors such as fine

◀ Guillemots crowd the ledges at Fowlsheugh

weather or just a particularly strong supply of food. The RSPB has now stepped up its monitoring to learn more.

From the interpretation board beyond the small car park, walk north along the cliff tops for 1km. There are plenty of benches to sit and watch the seabird world whirl by, while photographers will enjoy trying to capture full frame shots of many different species. Be sure to also scan the waters below for signs of marine life such as seals and bottlenose dolphins.

A smattering of puffins can sometimes be seen at the end of the trail, while the high vantage point is perfect for tracing the silvery outline of diving seabirds below. Like other members of the auk family, guillemots and razorbills have stubby wings designed more for underwater manoeuvring than flying. This means that taking off is rarely easy and the birds patter along the surface of the water in a frantic effort to gain lift.

For a different view of the seabird city, RSPB volunteers operate evening boat trips from Stonehaven harbour (May-July). Trips must be booked in advance from the RSPB East Scotland Regional Office.

Early birds

Black and white and found on less crowded ledges, razorbills can be heard making their low growling call along the tops of the Fowlsheugh cliffs. Like the guillemot, a close cousin, razorbills usually adopt a breeding strategy based on early departure of chicks – the premise being that food supplies are more predictable earlier in the season. As with most auks, the sheer strain of breeding means that the birds only attempt to raise one chick each season. The egg usually hatches in June and the chick remains on land for 21 days before leaving its ledge in mid-July. It is then cared for at sea by the male for up to two months.

Forvie Scottish Natural Heritage

Getting there **Waterside car park, 1.6km north of Newburgh on A975. Stevenson Forvie Centre near Collieston off B9003 (open year round, but check seasonal hours)** OS Map **Landranger 38**

A pristine dune system provides an ever-changing backdrop to mainland Scotland's largest gathering of breeding eider ducks.

Forvie's impressive dune system was created after the last Ice Age when retreating glaciers dumped huge volumes of sand in the area. A subsequent fall in sea level and plenty of gusting wind did the rest – as the medieval community of Forvie discovered to its cost when the settlement was overwhelmed by encroaching sand.

Today, the dunes provide a stunning, and still highly mobile, backdrop to a very different natural spectacle: mainland Scotland's largest gathering of breeding eider ducks. Although resident at Forvie all year round, eider numbers swell to nearly 5,000 between April and August.

During this time, these highly gregarious ducks can be seen feeding all along the lower Ythan estuary. Eiders have a particular liking for mussels – a preference that has seen them come into conflict with commercial mussel farmers elsewhere in Scotland. The molluscs, which grow in abundance on the estuary bed, are swallowed whole and ground into small pieces, leaving the banks crunchy underfoot from digested shells.

More than 2000 females nest in the heather and long grass, their mottled plumage providing camouflage from predators. Others chance more open sites,

Female eider on the nest

but not without risk: foxes, crows and gulls need no second invitation to take unguarded eggs.

And ducklings that do successfully hatch also risk being picked off by gulls as they dash from the heather to the water. Once there, eiders adopt the ultimate safety in numbers strategy: females organise and oversee large crèches of up to 100 ducklings, regardless of family origin.

In summer, the estuary also hosts up to 1000 pairs of sandwich tern and smaller numbers of Arctic, common and little tern. The terns nest on exposed areas of pebbles within the dunes where the chicks can also hide in the long marram grass.

Although the main ternery at the southern end of the reserve is fenced off during the summer breeding period, the birds are easily seen plunge diving for sandeels and small fish. For views across the mouth of the Ythan to the ternery, follow the road to the golf course alongside the Ythan Hotel and walk up into the dunes.

Visitors can also explore the reserve using three way-marked trails: a full day can be spent walking the coastal and estuary trails, both starting and finishing at the Waterside car park or the Stevenson Forvie Centre. The coastal trail is particularly impressive in early summer when the cliffs between Rockend and Collieston are awash with sea campion and other salt-tolerant plants.

Under the microscope

The Ythan estuary, which attracts large concentrations of birds year round, is one of the most studied habitats of its kind in Scotland. The mudflats can be viewed from various lay-bys along the A975, as well as a hide near the Bridge of Forvie. The estuary was the recent subject of the Ythan Project, a four-year initiative designed to highlight how the use of agri-environmental techniques by farmers and local landowners can prevent damaging run-off from leaching into the watercourse. This followed a worrying increase in growths of green macroalgae that can have a potentially serious impact on the wider estuary ecosystem.

◀ The mouth of the Ythan from Foveran Links

MONSTER MIDGE

Forming a rough triangle between the lowland plains of Kinross, the high tops of Creag Meagaidh and the remnant forest overlooking the Sound of Jura, the large area covered in this chapter includes a range of habitat with year round wildlife watching appeal.

Visitors to Vane Farm can see how wetland habitat is being managed to suit the needs of resident and migrant birds, while Loch of the Lowes (osprey) and Argaty (red kite) highlight charismatic species of raptor (birds of prey) once lost to Scotland, but now staging a comeback.

Elsewhere, the long-term regeneration of denuded landscapes at Ben Lawers and Creag Meagaidh continues to benefit specialist plant and animal communities, while Inversnaid offers a different

perspective on Scotland's best known loch – sometimes with wild goats for company.

This chapter ends with three west coast highlights: the dripping Atlantic oakwoods at Ariundle and Taynish – two of the best places to see otters on the Scottish mainland – and the sprawling raised bog at Moine Mhor. All three are known for their outstanding diversity of life and offer scope for multi-day explorations of surrounding areas.

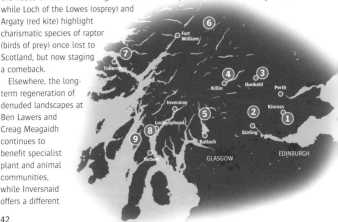

Southern, Central and West Highlands

Vane Farm RSPB Reserve

Getting there On B9097, 3.4km east of M90 near Kinross. Visitor centre (open year round). Admission charge OS Map Landranger 58

With thousands of wintering wildfowl and a growing number of nesting waders, Vane Farm offers year round appeal.

An important education resource for local schools and colleges, Vane Farm sits on the southern shore of Loch Leven – the largest body of water in lowland Scotland.

Part of the wider Loch Leven National Nature Reserve, this popular RSPB reserve covers a variety of habitat ranging from wet grassland along the loch shore to an area of mixed woodland that stretches to the summit of Vane Hill.

The fields in and around the reserve are a major wintering and staging point for thousands of geese (mainly pink-footed), drawn by the combination of a high winter water table and plenty of suitable grassland.

Much of the RSPB's past focus has been on maintaining suitable habitat for the geese, but this has since broadened to include a major effort to develop additional wetland suitable for breeding waders.

This has been achieved through the use of sluice gates that manipulate water levels to create a combination of shallow pools and muddy scrapes. The surrounding grassland is also cut for hay or silage in July and then grazed by Highland cattle to help form the kind of tussocky sward preferred by waders.

And results have been encouraging, with five species now breeding at Vane Farm: lapwing – the most numerous – snipe, redshank, oystercatcher and curlew.

Meanwhile, the observation room at Vane Farm offers a perfect window onto Loch Leven itself – one of Europe's most important inland sites for nesting ducks.

Although large in area, the loch is sufficiently shallow for swans and dabbling ducks to feed, while deeper parts are suitable for diving ducks.

St Serf's, the largest of the loch's seven islands, is a particular hive of activity in early summer: it holds more than 600 pairs of breeding tufted ducks, as well as significant numbers of mallard and shelduck.

Child's play

Originally intended for educational purposes and well used to catering for school groups, Vane Farm is an excellent place for children to learn more about the birds, animals and plants that inhabit this easily accessible reserve. The visitor centre is full of displays and interpretation, while the observation room is equipped with high-powered telescopes. Outside, a collection of hides, trails and ponds allow plenty of opportunity for exploring.

Although high summer is relatively quiet, Loch Leven's prized population of brown trout still attracts plenty of feeding osprey. The birds are often seen hunting over the loch in August and, occasionally, over the pools at Vane Farm.

From late summer, breeding birds make way for winter arrivals such as whooper swan, teal and a host of passage waders. Meanwhile, goose numbers begin to swell in September, peaking at around 14,000 in October before many head further south. They reappear in even greater numbers in mid-March ahead of a final push back to summer breeding grounds.

A well-equipped visitor centre provides panoramic views across the reserve, Loch Leven and surrounding hills, while three hides overlook the pools. For an even better perspective, follow the nearby woodland trail (2km) to the summit of Vane Hill.

Redshank are one of several breeding waders now doing well at Vane Farm

Argaty Red Kites

Getting there Feeding station and hide at Lerrocks Farm, near Stirling. Admission charge. Signposted from A84 at Doune
OS Map Landranger 57

This red kite feeding station offers exhilarating views of a magnificent bird of prey now finding its feet following reintroduction.

Once shot and poisoned to extinction in Scotland – and nearly lost completely in the UK – red kites have made steady progress since their initial reintroduction on the Black Isle in 1989.

Large and easily distinguished, with a characteristic forked tail, it was once assumed that kites posed a threat to pheasants and other game. This suspicion and the birds' vocal and inquisitive nature made them an easy target. The last breeding pair recorded in Scotland was in 1879.

However, following the inaugural Black Isle scheme, further reintroduction has seen dozens of birds brought in from Europe and released in central Scotland and later in Galloway.

Kites have long been considered an ideal candidate for reintroduction: despite an imposing five-foot wingspan, they are dainty birds built for gliding rather than brute strength, and live on a diet of carrion, topped up with worms and beetles.

Launched in November 2003 in partnership with the RSPB, the Argaty Red Kite venture allows remarkably close views of these graceful birds. It is one of two feeding stations in Scotland, the other being at Bellymack Hill Farm in Galloway.

Although food is provided year round, care is taken to avoid dependency: the food replicates carrion that the kites scavenge for naturally, while the same quantity is laid out regardless of season. Food is only provided in the afternoon, encouraging the birds to forage as normal in the morning.

A large hide, which can accommodate up to 30 people, overlooks the feeding area. Visitors can study the birds as they interact with other raptors attracted by the bounty: it is not unusual for a kestrel or sparrowhawk to be sitting quietly on a

◀ A red kite coming into feed at Lerrocks Farm

nearby post while the kites tussle with each other and the many buzzards circling overhead.

Usually first to feed, the buzzards play an important role: kites are not strong enough to rip open the food themselves and rely on the more powerful raptor to do this job for them. When ready, the kites swoop down amongst the buzzards, grabbing chunks of meat to eat on the wing.

While present year round, kites are most active in winter (Oct-March) when juveniles join adult birds in communal roosts. Up to 30 kites are attracted to the area, although as many as 80 have been seen on particularly lively days.

As this is a working farm, advance booking is always appreciated (details online). Visitors are either met at the car park or make their own way to the hide, a short way up a track. A knowledgeable guide provides interpretation while at the hide.

North and south

There has been a marked difference between the success of the Scottish red kite releases and those conducted at four sites across England. While more than 200 kite pairs now breed in the Chilterns in Oxfordshire, there are only around 35 pairs in the north of Scotland – despite starting from the same number of released birds. Sadly, illegal poisoning, whether intentional or indirect, remains a problem. Kite populations have, however, fared better in central Scotland and Galloway, with landowners and local communities actively supporting the birds. Here, low productivity is usually attributed to poor weather rather than anything more sinister.

Loch of the Lowes Scottish Wildlife Trust

Getting there **3km northeast of Dunkeld off A923 on minor road to Caputh. Visitor centre (open April-Sept). Admission charge** OS Map Landranger 52

Set in tranquil Perthshire countryside, Loch of the Lowes offers intimate views of breeding osprey and a variety of other wildlife throughout the year.

Potentially vulnerable wildlife is sometimes best observed in carefully managed circumstances and this is certainly the case at the Scottish Wildlife Trust's Loch of the Lowes visitor centre. Over a million visitors have witnessed the successful rearing of more than 60 chicks since osprey first bred here in 1969.

Two hides provide clear views to the osprey eyrie high in the trees across the loch. The birds can be seen not only at the nest – aided by a live camera feed – but also as they go about a daily routine of fishing, interacting with other species and even washing their talons in front of the hides.

Ospreys return from their West African wintering grounds in late March. The initial weeks are occupied with defending territories, nest refurbishment and mating. Usually three eggs are laid at short intervals in April with the chicks hatching, again at intervals, after almost 40 days. This sequential laying and hatching of eggs is designed to ensure the survival of the first born during times of food shortage.

The male bird supplies chicks with a steady diet of pike and perch plucked from the loch,

Return of the osprey

The recovery of Scotland's osprey population is a major conservation success story. The last birds were persecuted to extinction in Scotland in 1916 and osprey did not breed here again until the 1950s (at Loch Garten, near Aviemore). Numbers have since climbed to around 160 pairs, although the birds have not yet repopulated all of their old stomping grounds. Osprey often stay loyal to the area from which they fledge, so slowing their geographical spread. There are similar viewing centres at Loch Garten (see p72), in the Borders (Glentress Forest and Kailzie Gardens), the Trossachs (Aberfoyle) and Galloway (Wigton Bay).

Osprey with catch

as well as salmon and trout from the nearby River Tay. Osprey chicks grow fast and gain 80 per cent of their adult body weight during their first 30 days.

Within seven weeks, the chicks are ready to fly and can take their first fishing lessons – often an entertaining time to visit. The adult birds and juveniles leave the area, separately, in August or September.

But while the osprey family is the star attraction, the loch and surrounding mixed woodland also hold plenty of other wildlife throughout the year. Fallow and roe deer are often seen from the main hide (open all year), while a newly refurbished visitor

centre features a large viewing window where woodland birds such as great spotted woodpecker and siskin can be observed.

Red squirrels also frequent the feeders provided, while lucky visitors may even catch sight of an occasional otter. The loch itself has breeding great crested grebe in summer, often close to the hides.

As the largest of the five lochs in the area, Loch of the Lowes is the last to freeze in winter and so also attracts good numbers of wildfowl. Numbers build from September, peaking in early winter with up to 3000 migrant greylag geese roosting on the loch, as well as goldeneye, wigeon and teal.

◄ A placid Loch of the Lowes

Ben Lawers National Trust for Scotland

Getting there **Trails and visitor centre (open May-Sept), north side of Loch Tay on minor road off A827 near Edramucky. Admission charge** OS Map **Landranger 51**

Long-term efforts to restore rare arctic-alpine flora continue at one of the most botanically rich upland areas in the UK.

Ben Lawers is a dominant presence on the north side of Loch Tay: at 1,214m, it is not only the highest peak in the Southern Highlands, but also lends its name to a massif that includes six Munros along a series of high-level ridges.

It is here that a combination of lime-enriched rock, topology and climate has created conditions in which specialist montane scrub, moss, lichen and high-altitude flowering plant communities can flourish. And it is the rare mountain plants, in particular, that have drawn botanists to Ben Lawers since their discovery in the 18th century. Celebrated species include drooping saxifrage and Alpine gentian, as well as more common specimens such as moss campion and Alpine lady's mantle.

However, at least three centuries of heavy grazing by sheep and deer have greatly reduced the structure of the flower rich woodland that the area is able to support. Plant collecting has also taken its toll: the Highland saxifrage, the most endangered species on Ben Lawers, teetered on the brink of extinction – in part due to collecting – until a recent programme of propagation and planting.

Detailed monitoring by NTS, which manages the land in partnership with SNH,

The elusive wildcat

Solitary and territorial, the Scottish wildcat inhabits woodland and rocky hillsides up to around 450m. As with many upland areas north of the Central Belt, Ben Lawers is likely to hold small numbers, although actually spotting this most elusive of native mammals is another matter. Heavily built, with a thick, blunt tail and vertical black stripes down the body, wildcats are readily distinguished from domestic cats. Much more difficult, however, is identifying animals that have mated with domestic cats – a hybridisation that some conservationists fear will lead to the demise of what is considered a pure gene Scottish wildcat.

has created a better understanding of the practical measures required to reverse the decline. Walkers will spot several enclosed areas at different altitudes within which various species are being resurrected through natural regeneration and planting. With farmers retaining grazing rights on the hill and deer still numerous, the fences will remain for the time being.

Visitors can see what can be achieved when plant life is allowed to grow unhindered on a self-guided nature trail (1.75km) that climbs alongside the Edramucky Burn. This small but increasingly wild gully of patchy woodland highlights some of the plant species found only in sheltered areas and remote ledges higher up.

In summer, it is worth lingering to also enjoy the wildlife along the trail, including numerous dragonflies, butterflies and summer migrants such as meadow pipit, wheatear and skylark, as well as resident dippers.

The nature trail can be a warm-up for the much tougher trek to the summit of Ben Lawers itself and possible encounters with the area's upland wildlife: mountain hare and ptarmigan are sometimes spotted around the higher boulder fields, while red deer are numerous, but often better seen away from the busy paths in the sheltered coires below. NTS rangers also offer low-level guided walks in the summer.

◀ Flowering plants flourish along Edramucky Burn

51

Inversnaid RSPB Reserve

Getting there **East shore of Loch Lomond by Inversnaid Hotel. Access from minor road at Stronachlachar on B829 west of Aberfoyle** OS Map **Landranger 56**

Climbing steeply from the shores of Loch Lomond, this compact reserve is home to a variety of woodland wildlife – including a small herd of wild goats.

Nestled just off the West Highland Way long-distance walking route on the quieter east shore of Loch Lomond, the small RSPB reserve at Inversnaid offers a very different perspective on this well-used stretch of water.

Thick deciduous woodland rises steeply before emerging onto a more open landscape of crag and moor – a swift progression in habitat that can reveal a variety of wildlife, both resident and seasonal.

Summer migrants include good numbers of wood warbler, redstart and tree pipit, while redpoll also breed in the woods. Elsewhere, the burns that tumble down the hillside into the loch are home to common sandpiper, as well as year round residents such as dipper.

Preferring faster flowing stretches of water, dippers feed on aquatic invertebrates by walking along the bottom of burns and rivers, often against fierce currents. Their presence is usually a good indicator of water quality.

Higher up the slope, the thinning woodland edge habitat supports a small number of black grouse that have managed to maintain a foothold in the area. Volunteers recently planted more than 2000 Scots pine seedlings – part of a wider Scottish Forest Alliance initiative stretching

◀ Inversnaid from the west shore of Loch Lomond

over to Loch Katrine — that will provide future habitat for these vulnerable birds.

Elsewhere, the higher points on the reserve are good areas to scan for raptors: buzzard nest on the crags, while peregrine falcon, golden eagle and hen harrier can sometimes be spotted above clearer ground.

However, Inversnaid is not just about birds: pine marten are present in the woodland, although small numbers of red and roe deer are much more readily seen. Inversnaid is also one of several areas along Loch Lomond to hold small populations of wild goats (30-50 animals) — similar to isolated groups found in Galloway, the Borders and on west coast islands.

The animals that roam the hills around Loch Lomond are thought to originate from goats once kept as livestock but released to fend for themselves following the Clearances.

From Inversnaid Hotel, walk north along the West Highland Way for a few hundred metres before a short circular path (0.8km) begins a steep climb through the woodland.

Sharp-eyed visitors might spot some of the dozen pairs of pied flycatcher that breed in nest boxes erected along the trail, while photographers will also appreciate the panoramic views across the loch from the top of the trail — a good jumping off point for longer walks on the many fine hills in the area.

Wild goats roam many parts of Scotland

Creag Meagaidh Scottish Natural Heritage

Getting there Parking on north shore of Loch Laggan on A86 between Newtonmore and Roybridge OS Map Landranger 35

Long-term woodland regeneration is restoring tree and scrub cover to a once bare landscape – greatly benefiting wildlife along the way.

Woodland restoration is a desperately slow process, but such has been the progress at Creag Meagaidh over the past two decades that it is already possible to appreciate how the landscape has changed since the area first became a National Nature Reserve (NNR) in 1986.

Decades of heavy grazing by red deer and sheep had reduced the area's native woodland to just a few isolated pockets. However, with NNR status came a new approach to restoring the denuded tree cover: rather than adopt the traditional method of erecting fences to eliminate deer altogether, grazing pressure was reduced through culling the reserve's hind-dominated population to a level at which regeneration could occur.

As a result, a mosaic of different aged trees and mixed ground cover now stretches from the shores of Loch Laggan high into Coill a'Choire. Such restoration has come purely from the recovery of heavily browsed trees and self-seeding.

Higher still, the unbroken succession of vegetation continues with montane scrub and specialist lower plants around the high tops. Even the summit of Creag Meagaidh (1,128m) includes areas of woolly-fringe moss, a prime habitat for breeding dotterel.

Actual deer numbers on the reserve vary because of the transitory nature of the animals as they pass in and out of neighbouring estates. However, with an

Ptarmigan inhabit the high tops of Creag Meagaidh

emphasis on managing the habitat rather than the deer, there is no specific 'right' number of animals. Instead, SNH sets a desired annual cull of animals based on information from habitat monitoring, backed up by monthly deer counts.

Limited grazing has also created clearings that allow other vegetation to flourish – greatly benefiting woodland edge species such as black grouse. While chicks profit from the availability of invertebrate food in June and July, the lack of deer fences, a common cause of mortality amongst black grouse, has helped the adult birds.

From the car park at Aberarder, a clear path (6km) works its way up through the birch woodland to Lochan a' Choire (620m). Red deer can be seen on the hill, but are understandably wary given the level of culling over the years; the captive pen near the car park is often a better place to see them.

As the path rises, the dark crags of Creag Meagaidh slowly reveal themselves. While winter climbers tackle the huge buttresses head on, experienced walkers can skirt round the cliffs to access the high tops – home not only to dotterel in summer, but also mountain hare and ptarmigan year round.

Sika hybridisation

Initially introduced from Japan as a decorative species in the 1800s, sika deer have spread rapidly and are now present over at least a third of Scotland's red deer range – including small numbers at Creag Meagaidh. Sika stags, like hinds recognisable by their white rumps, readily mate with red deer and produce fertile offspring – a hybridisation that threatens the genetic integrity (and even appearance) of Scotland's 'pure' red deer. Widespread in the north of Scotland but more localised elsewhere, there are now only a handful of west coast islands that are completely free of sika or sika/red hybrids.

◄ Regenerating birch woodland

Ariundle Scottish Natural Heritage

Getting there **Trails lead from Forestry Commission's Airigh Fhionndail car park, 3km north of Strontian**
OS Map **Landranger 40**

Ariundle is an ideal starting point for exploring the wildlife – and cultural history – of the ancient broadleaved woodlands around Loch Sunart.

A remnant of the dense temperate woodland that once covered much of Europe's Atlantic coast, Ariundle's rain-soaked oakwoods provide a humid oasis for hundreds of primitive plants. Every boulder and fallen tree on the woodland floor is carpeted in mosses, ferns and liverworts in various shades of green.

However, man has greatly influenced the apparently natural structure and appearance of this and other oakwoods around Loch Sunart: down the centuries, heavy grazing, the use of oak as a valuable source of charcoal for iron smelting and the later encroachment of commercial conifer plantations have all contributed to the current composition of the woodland.

And the disparate areas of woodland are now entering another phase in their development through the Sunart Oakwoods Initiative – a partnership between private landowners, community groups and public bodies such as the Forestry Commission and SNH. The initiative aims to link the remnant areas of native woodland by harvesting conifer plantations, removing invasive rhododendrons and controlling grazing in the area.

A circular trail (4km) that starts at the Forestry Commission car park north of Strontian provides a snapshot of the kind of detailed habitat restoration underway. The trail, which runs alongside the River

Otters are nimble and adaptable hunters

Sunart's hidden depths

Almost 30km long and 120 metres deep in places, Loch Sunart's complex underwater topography hides a rich diversity of marine life, from cup corals to rare sponges. The rocky coastline also supports one of mainland Scotland's highest concentrations of otters. These charismatic animals hunt the kelp beds for butterfish and crabs and use the freshwater burns to wash sea salt from their fur – vital to maintain the buoyancy and insulation of their coat. Otters are sometimes spotted from the Garbh Eilean hide in the forest at Ardery (8km west of Strontian), although the seals that haul out on nearby skerries are a much more regular sight.

Strontian before entering Ariundle itself, includes a short loop that passes through some of Scotland's most primeval oakwood landscape.

While insects thrive in this lush environment, including more than 200 species of moth, the most prized inhabitant is the chequered skipper butterfly. This woodland edge species has disappeared from much of the UK, but retains a stronghold in oakwoods such as Ariundle. Chequered skippers can be seen on the wing here during May and June.

On warm days, also look out for slow worms basking by the side of the trail, while woodland birds such as great spotted woodpecker and treecreeper are all present.

Pine marten also live in the woods, but visitors are more likely to see their distinctive black droppings than the animals themselves. For close encounters with these mainly nocturnal mammals, head for the Ardnamurchan Natural History Centre at Glenmore, which includes a pine marten den amongst various exhibits on local wildlife.

Other fine oakwoods can also be explored while in the area: try the circular walk around Glenborrodale (an RSPB reserve) on the north shore of Loch Sunart, while a full day can be spent at the more remote Glencripesdale National Nature Reserve (best accessed by mountain bike) on the south shore.

◀ Lower plants carpet the woodland floor at Ariundle

Moine Mhor Scottish Natural Heritage

Getting there **Parking 3km south of Kilmartin on B8025 and at Dunadd Hill Fort, signposted off A816** OS Map **Landranger 55**

A natural relic in a glen peppered with ancient ruins, Moine Mhor is one of Scotland's finest examples of raised bog.

Studies on pollen samples taken from the underlying peat at Moine Mhor – Gaelic for Great Moss – indicate that the raised bog covering this part of Kilmartin Glen has been more than 5000 years in the making.

Once submerged beneath a brackish loch following the last Ice Age, the Moss has risen above the surrounding land through the gradual deposit and accumulation of dead plant matter. With little bacteria to aid composition, the dead plants have formed layers rather than decaying, and eventually compressed to form peat.

The upper, and living, part of the bog is dominated by a variety of multi-coloured sphagnum mosses that, like the peat beneath, are able to hold huge amounts of water. In between are the specialist plants that can live in such a sterile environment, from heather and sedges to strong-smelling bog myrtle.

Over the centuries, attempts have been made to drain sections of the Moss for various uses, but the focus now is on restoring the area to its natural state. Grazing is now confined to marginal areas, drainage channels have been dammed and encroaching birch and rhododendron cleared. Such measures have allowed water levels to rise, sphagnum mosses to repopulate drains and wildlife to flourish.

Riddled with hummocks and ditches, the Moss can be a hazardous place in which to walk, but poses little problem for the resident roe deer population. Deer tracks can be seen disappearing into the bog from the Tileworks Trail – a short path that leads

◀ The mouth of the River Add at Bellanoch

Birthplace of Scotland

Kilmartin Glen boasts an extraordinary collection of archaeological sites, from standing stones to burial chambers and rock carvings. Remarkably, there are more than 350 sites within a 10km radius of Kilmartin village, many of them prehistoric. Highlights include the ruined hillfort at Dunadd – dubbed the birthplace of Scotland – and the extensive prehistoric rock carvings at Achnabreck. Visit the Kilmartin House Museum for a detailed account of Scotland's richest archaeological landscape.

from the car park 3km south of Kilmartin.

During summer months, a variety of dragonflies hunt over the bog, while the plant life attracts butterflies such as large heath and Scotch argus. The area also holds a good population of raptors: buzzards are common year round, while osprey fish around the mouth of the meandering River Add. Hen harriers also hunt here and roost communally in winter amongst the heather.

Meanwhile, the estuary at Islandadd

Bridge provides an ideal feeding ground for waders and wildfowl, with autumn passage (Sept-Oct) a particularly busy time. While good views can be had from the Crinan Canal towpath, the area is best appreciated from the summit of Dunadd Hill, a rocky outcrop that rises out of the surrounding bog.

The capital of the 6th-century Celtic kingdom of Dalriada, Dunadd provides panoramic views over the Moss and west to the Paps of Jura.

The buzzard is Scotland's most common bird of prey

Taynish Scottish Natural Heritage

Getting there Small car park 1.6km down the Taynish Road, or walk in from Tayvallich village on B8025 OS Map Landranger 55

Tucked away on a remote peninsula, this dripping temperate rainforest combines secretive wildlife with striking views across several island chains.

Younger and less widespread than its tropical relative, temperate rainforests are found in only a handful of places around the world, including the west coast of Scotland. Although much diminished, Scotland's remnant patches of rainforest are hugely atmospheric and none more so than the ripe woodland found at Taynish.

Set on a narrow peninsula that juts into Loch Sween, Taynish contains a spine of mixed deciduous woodland that pours down to the shoreline. Here, the mild oceanic climate and 1500mm of average annual rainfall provide ideal conditions for the assortment of ferns, mosses and liverworts that blanket the trees and rocks.

The ancient oaks that dominate the tree cover play a vital role in the wider rainforest ecosystem, providing habitat for a huge number of organisms, including hundreds of insect species. The presence of such a rich source of food in turn attracts birds such as great spotted woodpecker and treecreeper, while the woodland also harbours buzzard, badger, roe deer and tawny owl.

However, man's use of the woodlands over the centuries has also ensured there are plenty of cleared areas and the reserve's patches of grazed grassland, wet meadows and bog also provide important habitat. In spring and summer, dragonflies hunt over the bogs, while the flower-rich meadows at the southern end of the peninsula are home

◄ Looking southwest over Loch Sween from Barr Mor

Beavers blocked

Conservationists were left surprised in 2005 when the Scottish Executive refused its own environment agency's licence application for a five-year trial reintroduction of European beavers at the Knapdale Wildlife Reserve near Taynish. SNH first began a national consultation on the proposed reintroduction in 1998, which received widespread public support. Despite SNH providing what it considered sound ecological and economic arguments for the trial, the Executive disagreed citing potential damage to a protected area of woodland as one concern. Beavers, a species hunted to extinction in Scotland 400 years ago, have been successfully reintroduced in more than 20 European countries.

to various species of butterfly and is a particular hotspot for the rare marsh fritillary.

The shoreline here also offers fine views across the tidal rapids to the Ulva Islands – an excellent area for shorebirds and exploring the plentiful marine life that is fed by the fast moving tides. As with much of Loch Sween, this is also prime otter territory: sitting quietly in a sheltered spot can pay dividends, particularly early or late in the day.

The reserve is accessed along a 5km circular trail that starts at the small SNH car park. The meadows and shoreline overlooking the tidal rapids are reached by a connecting coastal trail that passes close

to Taynish House, a private residence.

The main woodland trail also connects with a short but steep path to the bracken-strewn summit of Barr Mor: a wonderful place to watch the sun go down behind Jura and maybe even spot roe deer feeding amongst the bracken. Catch your breath on the way up by checking out the ruins of ancient hut platforms – later used as foundations for charcoal burners supplying the 19th-century iron-smelting industry.

The grey heron is a common shoreline bird

This chapter includes five entries located within the recently created Cairngorms National Park, a high mountain area to quicken the pulse of anyone with a love for the outdoors – and a hotspot for wildlife. Contained within the Park's boundaries are a variety of specialised habitats, from remnant Caledonian pinewoods to the Arctic tops of the Cairngorm plateau, that provide sanctuary for some of the UK's most impressive wildlife.

Sites such as Loch Garten (osprey, capercaillie) and Rothiemurchus (pine marten, badger) offer tailor-made facilities for viewing rare and elusive species, while others such as Glen Tanar and Glen Muick can be explored along a network of trails. Elsewhere, at Insh Marshes, the annual flooding of the Spey has created a sprawling wetland that attracts a variety of wintering and breeding birds.

Additional sites outside the National Park also contribute to the special nature of this part of Scotland. Loch Ruthven is the summer home of the spectacular slavonian grebe, while lonely Loch of Strathbeg is the first port of call for extraordinary numbers of pink-footed geese each autumn.

But perhaps best of all for many visitors is the chance to enjoy the Moray Firth's celebrated population of bottlenose dolphins – with the Whale and Dolphin Conservation Society's visitor centre at Spey Bay an excellent starting point.

Cairngorms and North-East Coast

Glen Muick

Getting there On minor road off B976 from
Ballater. Visitor centre (open year round).
Car park at Spittal of Glenmuick
OS Map Landranger 44

**Although one of the most visited parts
of the popular Balmoral estate, Glen
Muick still holds plenty of wildlife
interest – particularly for early risers.**

Tempting summits, royal connections and
ease of access mean that Glen Muick can
be a busy place. But while wildlife naturally
shrinks from the crowds during peak times,
many species show themselves more
readily at either end of the day.

Some of the best wildlife viewing can be
had from the narrow road that climbs up the
glen to a car park near Loch Muick. Brown
hare frequent the agricultural land up to
around 300m, after which the road opens

out onto managed moorland – territory
much better suited to mountain hare.

Prone to wild fluctuations in numbers,
mountain (or blue) hare mostly lie low
during the day to avoid predators such as
golden eagle, but can be seen feeding near
the road at dusk or early in the morning.
When there is good snow cover, the hares'
white winter coats provide perfect
camouflage, but can make them dangerously
conspicuous during milder periods.

Meanwhile, the woodland edges in the
lower glen also provide prime habitat for
black grouse – a species that continues to
struggle in parts of Scotland, but has
prospered across Deeside in recent years.
In Glen Muick itself, the population has
benefited from the removal and marking of
many kilometres of deer fencing (often the
cause of fatal collisions) as well as

◄ Pinewood stand at the Spittal of Glenmuick

predator control linked with the estate's wider moorland management for red grouse.

In spring and early summer, the boggy moorland further up the glen is full of the distinctive sights and sounds of displaying wading birds; curlew, golden plover and lapwing all breed here, while snipe can be seen guarding their broods from the tops of rocks.

However, Glen Muick is perhaps best known for its red deer: the animals are often seen from the roadside, while a small herd of bachelor stags loiter around the Spittal bog (between the visitor centre and Loch Muick). The animals tolerate a reasonably close approach and are best viewed from just after the October rut through to spring, when most head for higher ground to escape the attention of midges and other biting insects.

A walk around Loch Muick (12km) offers a good low-level introduction to the plants and animals of this grand landscape – including the towering bulk of nearby Lochnagar (1155m). Trail maps are available from the visitor centre, as are details of ranger-led walks. Be sure to look out for the red squirrels that frequent the nut feeders nearby.

Managing for grouse

A plump game bird of upland bogs and heather moorland, red grouse are a familiar sight to many walkers: the birds often explode noisily from dense cover – sometimes close enough to spot the red combs over the male birds' eyes. Somewhat perversely, grouse shooting – a mainstay of many estates – appears to also provide direct benefits for the conservation of other upland wildlife. Moorland maintained for red grouse through muirburn (to stimulate new growth), predator control and other measures frequently hold high densities of breeding wading birds, such as lapwing, dunlin and curlew.

Glen Tanar

Getting there Car park, trails, visitor centre (open year round, check seasonal hours) at Braeloine, 2.5km along estate road. Access from Bridge o' Ess on B976
OS Map Landranger 44

Forest regeneration efforts at Glen Tanar estate continue to benefit some of Scotland's most precious species.

Bordered by the River Dee in the north and Mount Keen to the south, Glen Tanar estate contains a prized mix of forest and moorland habitat. The forest, which follows the course of the Tanar and its tributaries to an altitude of 450m, includes areas of aspen, birch and oak, but is dominated by native Caledonian pinewood.

With the estate owner's land management policy having long focused on the regeneration of this Caledonian forest, Glen Tanar is blessed with mosaics of even age trees and an unusually wide range of age classes.

Elsewhere, regeneration continues with deer control central to the wider effort. In the past, this was achieved through the use of fences as a protective shield. However, such a solution often creates an artificial looking environment – with fenced stands of forest next to heavily grazed areas – and recent efforts have concentrated instead on creating a more natural landscape.

Many kilometres of fencing have now been removed, while the estate has adopted an increasingly scientific approach to monitoring the impact of deer and culling accordingly.

Fence removal has also benefited vulnerable pinewood species such as capercaillie. This huge woodland grouse tends to fly low and fast when disturbed, increasing the chance of collision.

◄ Regenerating pinewood at Glen Tanar

Detailed studies have pinpointed which fences need to be removed, or at least made more visible.

The birds also require a range of habitat, including dense thicket for shelter and open woodland for food. A healthy under storey of blaeberry is of particular importance: the plant provides a source of insects for chicks, while adults feed on its shoots and berries.

However, with a management programme aimed at controlling deer impact, bracken and heather can easily become overgrown, impeding the growth of blaeberry. To combat this, the estate is currently involved in an EU LIFE pilot programme to develop capercaillie habitat, which includes prescribed burning of overgrown areas. Early reports are promising: blaeberry has returned to many cleared parts of the forest and there is sign of capercaillie activity.

The ranger service organises groups – such as the John Muir Trust – to assist in such habitat work and the estate is keen to extend its volunteer programmes. Such a hands-on role offers the chance of spotting capercaillie and other pinewood specialities such as Scottish crossbill and red squirrel.

Elsewhere, hen harrier and golden eagle regularly hunt over open ground, while the estate's many miles of trails provide ample opportunity for exploring an area that rewards patient discovery.

Black grouse stronghold

In addition to promising numbers of capercaillie, Glen Tanar has traditionally been a stronghold for black grouse, another distinctive species known for its spectacular dawn mating display (or lek). An upland bird of woodland fringes, black grouse have also benefited from the removal of deer fencing, as well as efforts to create a more natural edge between forest and open moorland. The birds can sometimes be seen along the estate's trails, particularly the main track running past Etnach – a welcome sign for a species showing a worrying decline elsewhere in Scotland.

Insh Marshes RSPB Reserve

Getting there **On B970 near Ruthven Barracks, 2km from Kingussie. Hides and trails** OS Map **Landranger 35**

An important natural floodplain wetland, the sprawling Insh Marshes occupies a striking position between the Monadh Liath mountains and the Cairngorm plateau.

The priority with most UK rivers is to build defences that control water levels and reduce the risk of flooding. Not so at Insh Marshes where the Spey is left to flood through natural breaches in the riverbank, often creating a near perfect moat around the nearby Ruthven Barracks.

Traditionally triggered by surges of spring melt water from the hills, the flooding now increasingly occurs following periods of heavy rain at other times of year. This natural fertilising of the land attracts large numbers of wildfowl, with wigeon, teal and greylag geese all prevalent from October to March. The marshes and nearby Loch Insh also hold up to 150 whooper swans that arrive to feed each winter from Iceland.

Large numbers of breeding waders join the throng in spring together with almost half of Britain's population of breeding goldeneye. A medium-sized diving duck, goldeneye normally nest in holes in mature trees. However, with a shortage of natural sites the ducks have taken to breeding in nest boxes erected in the surrounding birch woodland and on riverside trees.

Once born, the ducklings wait to fluff up for 24 hours before being marched to the

Goldeneye taking off

water by their mothers. The ducklings usually fledge in late May, but face many hazards before doing so: pine marten predation of nest sites can be high, while otter and pike both present a hazard once on the water.

During drier summers, the floodwater retreats leaving a patchwork of isolated lochans and oxbow lakes. Sheep and cattle graze the area, performing the vital job of preventing the marshes from becoming overgrown. Roe deer are found across the reserve, while the meadows that make up much of the area are home to more than 500 species of plant, from field gentians to spotted orchids.

Meanwhile, rabbit-proof fencing protects stands of aspen and birch woodland, which in turn provides habitat for a range of insects, mosses and fungi.

The reserve itself has two hides, an information viewpoint and a circular trail, all of which are accessible from the main car park. The picnic area on the glacial escarpment above Invertromie Farm is a good place to scan for hen harrier and geese in winter, as well as osprey later in the year.

The car park also marks the start of the Badenoch Way, a 16-km trail that heads north towards Aviemore. Additional, shorter walks can be accessed from nearby Insh village and alongside the loch itself.

Scotland's past and present

Managed by the Royal Zoological Society of Scotland, the nearby Highland Wildlife Park is dedicated to showcasing Scotland's most important species, both past and present. In the main reserve, visitors are given an interpretive CD to play as they drive amongst free-ranging Highland cattle, red deer, European bison and elk. Elsewhere, various walk-through areas highlight particular habitats and the wildlife that inhabit them. This includes several species long extinct in the wild in Scotland, such as wolf and lynx, plus more elusive present-day wildlife, including wildcat and pine marten.

◀ Flooded meadows surround a glacial island at Insh Marshes

Rothiemurchus

Getting there **Between Aviemore and the Cairngorm ski centre. Visitor centre (open year round) on A951 at Inverdruie**
OS Map **Landranger 36**

Rothiemurchus offers a cross-section of the diverse habitat that makes Speyside such a hotspot for many iconic species.

Sandwiched between Aviemore and the Cairngorm ski centre, Rothiemurchus estate plays a key role in the economic development of an area often considered the 'outdoor capital' of Scotland. Although known for its diversified land use and historical importance, it is the estate's natural heritage that is its greatest draw.

The estate stretches from the banks of the Spey to the summit of Braeriach almost 1300m up on the Cairngorm plateau. Such a swift progression from riverbank to high montane habitat provides conditions for a celebrated roll call of wildlife – from otters along the river, to dotterel, ptarmigan and mountain hare on the high tops.

Central to the estate's conservation-minded operation is the gradual regeneration of one of Scotland's most significant remaining fragments of old Caledonian pinewood. Starting in nearby Abernethy, this chunk of ancient forest runs contiguously through Rothiemurchus south to Glen Feshie. Over the centuries, a combination of heavy grazing by sheep and deer – the latter unchecked by natural predators – plus strong demand for timber during wartime seriously depleted the Caledonian forests.

And there is much to conserve: the old forest is home to classic Speyside species such as crested tit, Scottish crossbill and pine marten. Red squirrels are also enjoying something of a renaissance, although remain

Cairngorm reindeer

The Cairngorms' range of wildlife includes Britain's only free ranging herd of reindeer. Having been lost in the wild in Scotland, the animals were reintroduced by Mikel Utsi, a Swedish reindeer herder, in 1952. Today, around 130 animals roam the hills, although roughly half have been relocated to a second site near Tomintoul. Visits to the herd leave the Cairngorm Reindeer Centre in Glenmore Forest Park daily throughout the year (twice daily in summer). Although the animals are extremely tame, walkers should avoid bulls if encountered on the hill during the October rut.

at high risk from traffic on the roads.

Capercaillie, another flagship species, are also doing better here than in many parts of Scotland, but remain particularly vulnerable to disturbance. Visitors wishing to see the spectacular dawn mating display (or lek) of these impressive birds should head for the RSPB's dedicated viewing site at nearby Loch Garten (April-May).

Meanwhile, badger and pine marten numbers are increasing, while the local osprey population makes full use of easy pickings at the Rothiemurchus fishery at Inverdruie. From April onwards, adults can be seen snatching rainbow trout from the well-stocked lochs.

One of the best ways to see wildlife in Rothiemurchus is to take an early morning walk along one of the estate's huge network of tracks, or make a dawn visit to Loch an Eilein. Rangers also offer guided walks throughout the year.

For a more intimate experience, partner organisation Speyside Wildlife operates bespoke, guided daytrips, as well as year-round access to a large night viewing hide in the forest. The glass-fronted facility offers an excellent opportunity to see pine marten, badgers and other elusive mammals at extremely close quarters. Booking is essential, either online or through the Rothiemurchus Visitor Centre.

◂ Rothiemurchus estate from Craigellachie

Loch Garten RSPB Reserve

Getting there 16km east of Aviemore between Boat of Garten and Nethybridge, off B970. Osprey Centre (open April-Aug). Admission charge OS Map Landranger 36

Breeding osprey and capercaillie are the star turns at this famous site deep within Scotland's largest remnant of ancient Caledonian forest.

For 50 years, the name Loch Garten has been synonymous with the return of breeding osprey to Scotland. It was here in 1954 that the species first bred after a lengthy absence and, despite a shaky start, subsequent pairs have raised more than 70 young – to the delight of thousands of visitors each year.

Today, the birds' eyrie is overlooked by a purpose-built Osprey Centre; a combination of telescopes, CCTV images and expert interpretation provides visitors with a rare insight into the behaviour of this fish-eating raptor.

Each year, Loch Garten staff wait anxiously to see if the previous season's adults make it back from their West African wintering grounds (usually late March) and what interaction there might be with other ospreys returning to the area.

The Osprey Centre only opens to the public once the pair has settled in and begun the breeding process. By late-May, a clutch of up to four eggs has usually hatched allowing visitors to chart the development of the osprey chicks up to their first flight in mid- to late-July. During this period, the male osprey can be seen returning to the nest with a steady supply of pike and trout.

Meanwhile, the area around Loch Garten

Cock capercaillie at the lek

also holds plenty of other pinewood specialities, with red squirrel, crested tit and Scottish crossbill all seen around the Osprey Centre and nearby trails. Best of all, for a six-week period each spring, the Osprey Centre doubles as a viewpoint for watching cock capercaillie lekking in the forest bog surrounding the osprey eyrie.

RSPB staff run dawn capercaillie watches during the peak period of activity (1 April-21 May). For once, the ospreys perched nearby play second fiddle as visitors relish this rare opportunity to witness the dramatic breeding display of this enormous woodland grouse without fear of disturbance. Views are sometimes distant and fleeting, but no less impressive for it.

Sadly, the capercaillie is in genuine danger of extinction in Scotland (for the second time): there are now less than 1000 individuals left in the wild, with almost 15 per cent of the population inhabiting the pinewoods of the surrounding Abernethy Forest.

Although the birds lek over an extended period, hens only come to the cocks on a handful of mornings. However well intentioned, it is unwise (and now illegal) for visitors to seek out lekking capercaillie during this crucial period – particularly when such a discreet viewing facility is readily available.

Captive breeding

Efforts to boost capercaillie numbers include several captive breeding programmes run in affiliation with the Royal Zoological Society of Scotland. One such project began at Aigas Field Centre near Beauly in autumn 2004 with the arrival of four adult birds (used as breeding stock) from the Highland Wildlife Park. Successfully reared birds will be available for restocking in the wild. Similar initiatives have been tried elsewhere in the past, but foundered when lack of suitable habitat and associated predation saw the birds fail to breed in the wild – crucial points that the Field Centre and conservation bodies are addressing with landowners.

Loch Ruthven RSPB Reserve

Getting there **Signposted off B851 at East Croachy, 25km southwest of Inverness** OS Map **Landranger 26**

Sheltered by craggy hills and fringed by birch woodland, this isolated loch is the UK's most important site for breeding slavonian grebe.

While tourists flock to nearby Loch Ness to catch sight of a certain mythical creature, wildlife watchers seek out something much more tangible, but almost as exotic, at a less grand stretch of water. Each year (April-Aug), Loch Ruthven is home to the UK's largest gathering of slavonian grebes – perhaps the most striking of all Scotland's breeding birds.

Although grebes winter off the Scottish coast in the hundreds, they remain a rare and localised summer breeder, preferring just a handful of lochs and wetland areas

around the Great Glen and Strathspey. Relatively dull in their black and white winter plumage, the birds come alive in summer with their red eyes set against a wild head plume of gold and burnt orange flanks.

Although difficult to pinpoint when the birds first came to Loch Ruthven, they have used the loch in significant numbers since at least the 1930s. In recent years, Ruthven has held as many as 27 pairs during one season, although closer to 20 pairs is more usual. This equates to around half of Scotland's fluctuating breeding population and about two-thirds of the young – which can be seen riding on their parents' backs from mid-June.

The birds are attracted to the loch for a combination of reasons: the extensive sedge beds that fringe the loch provide an ideal nest site, while the unpolluted water

◄ Farmland around Loch Ruthven

holds plenty of prey items such as minnows, sticklebacks and insect larvae. Crucially, there are no mink in the area – an arrival that would devastate not only the grebes, but many other breeding species on and around the loch.

The birds are happy to nest in high density – often close to the shore – with up to four or five pairs in just one small area of sedge. Such close breeding provides a certain safety in numbers. Others nest near to noisy gull colonies elsewhere on the loch, which also provides a measure of predator control.

Reasonably confiding, the grebes can be seen from the 1km path that runs from the car park through the woods to a hide overlooking the loch. This is also a good spot to enjoy other summer visitors: red-throated and black-throated divers feed here on a regular basis – their eerie calls sometimes echoing across the loch – as does the local population of ospreys.

Grebe predation

Scotland's slavonian grebes have traditionally suffered not only lower breeding productivity compared with other European populations, but also higher predation of adult birds. To learn more, the RSPB rigged up miniature 24-hour cameras next to several nests to check the frequency and source of predation. It was found that some egg losses were caused by desertion and removal of eggs by incubating grebes, while otters were also seen to predate at egg, chick and adult stage, although not at particularly high levels. Of much more concern was the impact of flooding and wave action, particularly on nests in more exposed parts of the loch.

Slavonian grebe in breeding plumage

Spey Bay Whale and Dolphin Conservation Society

Getting there **WDCS wildlife centre at Tugnet on B9104, 9km from Fochabers**
OS Map Landranger 28

Home to the Whale and Dolphin Conservation Society, Spey Bay offers an ideal introduction to the marine life of the wider Moray Firth.

Housed in a former salmon fishing station at the mouth of the Spey, the Whale and Dolphin Conservation Society's (WDCS) wildlife centre is a good starting point for learning about the whales, dolphins and porpoises (or cetaceans) that inhabit the Moray Firth.

Although several species of cetacean use these waters, the Moray Firth is best known for its year round population of bottlenose dolphins. This isolated group of around 130 individuals is one of just two such resident populations in the UK – the other being at Cardigan Bay in Wales.

As with populations elsewhere in the world, food supply is a major factor in determining both school size and range. Although flexible, the dolphins concentrate on nutritious staples such as salmon, bass and mackerel and are equally adept at hunting individually, or working together to corral fish to the surface of the water.

The Moray Firth dolphins comprise two interconnected social groups: a large school that remains within the inner firth year round and a smaller, increasingly transient group that ranges up and down the east coast. It is not uncommon for animals to be sighted as far south as the Firth of Forth.

During the spring and summer, WDCS volunteers conduct hourly shore watches around Spey Bay to monitor dolphin

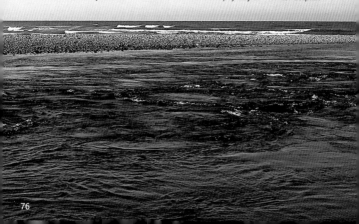

Bottlenose dolphin and calf

Close encounters

Chanonry Point is by far the best of the many land-based dolphin-watching locations along the Moray Firth. Situated on the Black Isle near Fortrose (OS Map Landranger 27), it marks the point where two peninsulas come together to form a narrow, but very deep channel. The dolphins ambush fish as they are funnelled through by the changing tides – sometimes close enough to splash people watching just metres away on the shore. Even when not actively fishing, the dolphins are often seen interacting as they wait for the tide to deliver food. In summer, the first couple of hours after low tide can provide particularly memorable moments.

behaviour, while survey boats are also used to maintain a detailed photographic record. Each individual is identified by the unique nicks and scrapes on its sickle-shaped dorsal fin and along its flanks.

WDCS staff can recommend many land-based dolphin-watching sites along the Moray Firth, while several boat operators sail from nearby Lossiemouth and Buckie. The whole experience is much better (for both visitors and dolphins) if trips are booked with operators accredited to the Dolphin Space Programme – a code of conduct drawn up to minimise disturbance to these vulnerable animals.

Meanwhile, the mouth of the Spey itself – a Scottish Wildlife Trust nature reserve – is also worth exploring further, and not just for the dolphins. Here, the violent confluence of river and sea has created the largest vegetated shingle beach system in Scotland.

Home to a rich assemblage of plants, the shingle supports sea duck throughout the year and provides nest sites for breeding waders and terns. Osprey also fish here on a regular basis during the summer.

Visitors can walk the shingle beach, or take on some of the Speyside Way – a long-distance footpath (135km) that follows the river inland to Aviemore.

◀ The mouth of the Spey at Tugnet

Loch of Strathbeg RSPB Reserve

Getting there **1.6km north of Crimond,
signposted from A90. Visitor centre
(open year round) Hides and trails**
OS Map **Landranger 30**

**Attractive wetland and an exposed
coastal location make Loch of
Strathbeg an important staging post
for vast numbers of migrating and
wintering birds.**

A dune slack loch – the largest of its kind
in the UK – Loch of Strathbeg is separated
from the North Sea by a narrow channel,
itself connected to a tidal lagoon amongst
the dunes. Fringed by marsh, fen woodland
and extensive reed beds, the loch provides
outstanding wetland habitat for a huge
variety of birds.

Keen birdwatchers recognise this RSPB
reserve as a top site for passage waders,
with ruff, black-tailed godwit and
greenshank all passing through (spring and
autumn), plus a steady flow of rarities.

General wildlife enthusiasts, however,
cannot help but be impressed by the sheer
number of birds that descend here in
autumn – in particular, the thousands of
pink-footed geese that arrive from their
Icelandic breeding grounds.

Goose numbers usually peak in October –
with recent highs topping 60,000 birds –
before dropping to a more steady 20,000 for
the remainder of the winter. Overall, a
remarkable 60 per cent of the world
population of pink-footed geese spend time
on and around the reserve during this period.

Such large numbers mean that Loch of
Strathbeg is one of several sites across
Scotland involved in a goose management
scheme drawn up to minimise potential

Roe deer buck

Secrets of the roe deer

Although birds dominate at Loch of Strathbeg, there is plenty of other wildlife interest including scattered groups of roe deer – often seen in the marshy woodland around the fen hide. Highly adaptable, roe deer prefer woodland habitat that affords permanent cover, but are now found increasingly on open moorland. Much smaller than red deer, roes are a reddish-brown in summer and quite grey in winter. During the rut – from mid-July to August – the males (or bucks) are aggressive defenders of territory, often barking at and chasing away competitor animals.

conflict with local farmers. Financed and administered by SNH, the scheme sees farmers receive payments for managing their land in a way that supports large numbers of geese, but also minimises damage to agriculture.

The pink-foots are joined by barnacle geese from Svalbard and hundreds of whooper swans. Meanwhile, the reed beds provide cover for wintering ducks and are one of the few regular wintering sites in Scotland for bittern – an elusive species often best seen near the fen hide when the loch freezes over.

Although quieter, spring and summer are also good times to visit: lapwing and redshank breed on the wet grassland, while arable land farmed on the reserve attracts

corn bunting, yellowhammer and skylark. Elsewhere, common terns nest on manmade islands and rafts in front of the visitor centre and near the bay hide.

However, one of the summer highlights for many visitors is the reserve's handful of breeding great crested grebes. A handsome species, with an elaborate courtship display, the bird was once widely hunted for its ornate feathers, but has become an established breeding species at Loch of Strathbeg.

The reserve has four hides in total, although three are reached through a nearby MoD airfield. As access arrangements can change, it is best to check first at the visitor centre (which also provides directions and trail guides).

◀ Reed beds and open water around the fen hide

To journey north from the Great Glen up through Wester Ross and into northwest Sutherland is to experience a landscape of intimidating scale – and great natural beauty. Solitary peaks thrust out of the surrounding moorland, while the battered coastline is marked by deep sea lochs, towering cliffs and some of the most pristine beaches imaginable.

This chapter provides a snapshot of the equally remarkable wildlife that inhabits this stunning region, including two sites on the gentler east coast: Nigg and Udale Bays on either side of the Cromarty Firth and the large tidal basin at Loch Fleet.

Both are excellent spots for viewing a variety of life from fishing osprey to loafing common seals.

Meanwhile, upland wildlife such as pine marten and black-throated diver can be encountered at Glen Affric and Beinn Eighe – two areas also known for their impressive cover of ancient Caledonian pinewood.

Further north is the wonderful Handa Island, one of the UK's most important seabird stations, as well as two destinations that could not be more different: picturesque Faraid Head, with its easily accessible puffins, and Forsinard, the waterlogged and unforgiving home of some of Scotland's hardiest plants and animals.

Northern Highlands

Glen Affric Forestry Commission Scotland

Getting there 8km west of Cannich on the Glen Affric road, off A831. Various car parks and trails along the glen
OS Maps Landranger 25 and 26

The sweeping Caledonian pinewoods of Glen Affric can be explored along a variety of scenic trails – with countless opportunities for wildlife watching along the way.

Together with Cannich and Strathfarrar, Glen Affric forms a triumvirate of classic Highland glens that cut deep into Strathglass west of Loch Ness. A National Nature Reserve managed by Forestry Commission Scotland, Glen Affric contains a now thriving remnant of native Caledonian pinewood, the core area of which has been under close conservation management since the 1960s.

The slopes on the south side of the River Affric, in particular, are covered in a glorious sweep of forest characterised by a wide variety of species and good age range from saplings to 'granny' pines and plenty of dead wood.

Specialist boreal species are well represented on the woodland floor, with rowan, juniper, blaeberry and various flowering plants creating the kind of rich understorey that plays such a vital role in the wider forest ecosystem.

Although typical pinewood wildlife can be found throughout the forest, some species are doing better than others. Osprey fish on the lochs and there is a healthy population of black grouse, but capercaillie are only present in low numbers, despite the much-improved habitat. Some point the finger at predation by pine marten, a renascent species in Glen Affric, although a combination of factors, including poor weather at the vital egg and chick stage, is probably just as likely.

Much of Affric's wildlife is best seen by exploring the trails that lead from various

◄ Dog Falls in the heart of Glen Affric

parking areas along the glen. The Dog Falls car park is a particularly good starting point, with several walks – Dog Falls (3.2km), Viewpoint (3.2km) and Coire Loch (5.2km) – fanning out into the core forest.

Of the three, the Coire Loch walk is particularly good for spotting pinewood birds and mammals. As well as pine marten, look out for red squirrel, Scottish crossbill and crested tit, while there are several distinctive woodant nests along the way. These large mounds – up to a metre high – are constructed from pine needles and twigs at the foot of trees, usually at the edge of open areas of woodland.

Meanwhile, Coire Loch itself is the breeding ground for many species of dragonfly and damselfly, while goldeneye and red-throated divers use this and other lochans in spring and early summer.

Elsewhere, the River Affric car park at the western end of the public road is a popular jumping-off point for longer excursions – with many walkers using the remote youth hostel at Alltbeithe for a welcome break.

Back from the brink

The pine marten has enjoyed quite a comeback in Scotland over the past decade: once hunted for their pelts and later by gamekeepers, the animal is now protected and has returned across much of its former range. Expert tree climbers, pine martens hunt a variety of prey from small mammals to frogs and birds. In summer, when the blaeberry is out, the animals gorge themselves on the abundant berries – leaving bright purple scat in prominent places. Although mainly nocturnal, pine martens are sometimes seen on trails early in the morning and also visit Glen Affric's picnic areas looking for scraps.

A clambering pine marten

Nigg and Udale Bays RSPB Reserves

Getting there **Nigg Bay, Easter Ross**
– hide 1.6km north of Nigg village off
B9175. Udale Bay, Black Isle – hide 1.5km
west of Jemimaville on B9163
OS Map **Landranger 21**

**Pioneering coastal realignment work has
added to the variety of life found amidst
the oil platforms of the Cromarty Firth.**

Facing each other across a firth often
dotted with oil platforms, the estuarine bays
of Nigg and Udale dispense with the idea
that wildlife and heavy industry are unable
to coexist.

With the whole of the Cromarty Firth
designated a Special Protection Area, the oil
industry is necessarily vigilant and there
appear to be no ill effects: otters are present
on the estuary and bottlenose dolphins are
often spotted from the headlands of the
nearby North and South Sutors.

Meanwhile, the sheltered inter-tidal sand
and mudflats at Nigg and Udale are alive with
activity, particularly between mid-September
and March when they provide food and
shelter for thousands of wintering birds.

Waders such as redshank, dunlin and bar-
tailed godwit forage for invertebrates, while
the abundant eelgrass exposed at low tide
attracts thousands of wigeon and smaller
numbers of mute and whooper swans.
Many birds use the flats to fuel up before
heading further south, while others remain
the whole winter.

Both bays cover large areas and the best
views are had for an hour or two either side
of high tide when the birds are pushed up
close to the shore. Of the two, Udale is of
more manageable size with a lay-by and
nearby hide that provide excellent views,
often regardless of the tide time. It is also
worth exploring along the minor road to

◄ Looking south across Nigg Bay at dusk

Balblair that starts near a ruined church.

Meanwhile, Nigg Bay – situated further north in Easter Ross and also with a hide overlooking the flats – gained national attention in 2003 when it was the subject of Scotland's first coastal realignment project. The aim was to recreate areas of saltmarsh, mudflat and wet grassland in an effort to mitigate for wintering bird habitat lost through land reclamation and rises in sea level.

The project saw a breaching of coastal defences in two places, allowing the sea to flood into the previously drained grassland behind; with each tide, the sea has gradually deposited fine layers of mud, full of invertebrates. Already, several species of saltmarsh plants have taken root, while a variety of ducks and waders have been tempted in from the wider estuary.

It is hoped that as the layers of mud build up, so more species will gradually use the area. Cost-effective and wildlife friendly, this kind of coastal realignment also offers a more natural way of creating a buffer zone to protect coastal communities.

Leap of faith

Visitors to the Falls of Shin – a short drive north of Nigg Bay on the B864 – can witness an iconic moment in the Scottish wildlife calendar: leaping Atlantic salmon. Having spent several winters at sea, the adult salmon return to their freshwater birthplaces to spawn for the first time – a fraught enough journey that, in this case, includes negotiating these formidable falls. The fish do so by contracting anaerobic muscles to generate intense bursts of speed that can propel them up even a waterfall of this size. However, if the leap fails, it can take the fish many hours to summon sufficient energy for a second attempt. The salmon are at their most lively in February and September.

Loch Fleet Scottish Wildlife Trust

Getting there **8km north of Dornoch off A9. South shore accessed along minor road to Skelbo. North shore accessed off Golspie to Littleferry road** OS Map **Landranger 21**

An attractive tidal basin that is a favourite fishing ground for osprey in summer and home to a year-round colony of common seals.

The last in a series of estuaries on Scotland's northeast coast, Loch Fleet has changed much in character over the centuries. Once an open sea loch stretching 6km inland, this large tidal basin morphed into its current form when shingle deposited across the loch entrance gradually reduced its contact with the Moray Firth to just a narrow channel.

More recently, the Mound causeway – completed by Thomas Telford in 1818 and which now supports the A9 – acts as a tidal barrier, blocking the sea 2km short of its natural range. Today, it also marks the western edge of the Loch Fleet National Nature Reserve.

As the largest single area of habitat on the reserve, the tidal basin is the focus of much of the wildlife activity. At low tide, a group of common seals (50-70 individuals) regularly haul out on sandbanks often close enough to the southern shore to hear them exhale.

There is also bird life everywhere: in summer, oystercatcher and redshank feast on the thousands of invertebrates that inhabit the inter-tidal flats, while eider ducks enjoy the mussel beds north of the river channel.

Common seal resting at low tide

Seal cycles

Unlike grey seals, which decamp to remote beaches and rocky island coves to breed (Sept-Dec), common seals are much less tied to the land during the breeding season. Common pups are born in June and join their mothers in the water almost from birth. Mating occurs after weaning and in both species the development of the embryo is suspended for four months following conception. After implantation, gestation continues for seven months with the birth coinciding with the correct season for each species – summer for commons and autumn for greys.

In autumn, dunlin and bar-tailed godwits join local populations of greylag geese to feed and roost on the loch – often bolstered by several thousand Icelandic greylags – before many species move further south. Wader and wildfowl numbers build up again in spring ahead of return trips back to summer breeding grounds.

Elsewhere, the north of the reserve contains two plantations of Scots pine, with the older of the two, Balblair Wood, holding specialised ground flora more typical of ancient Caledonian pinewoods. Balblair specialities include creeping lady's-tresses and twinflower wintergreen, while it also holds 90 per cent of the UK population of one-flowered wintergreen.

For non-botanists, summer is also an excellent time to visit: there are Scottish crossbill in the pinewoods, while Loch Fleet is a wonderful site to watch fishing osprey – a species that has bred successfully here in recent years.

The car park near Skelbo Castle (on the south side) can produce stunning views as the birds pluck flounder and sea trout from the loch. Elsewhere, the Mound pool car park at the northern end of the causeway is also good for fishing osprey.

Additional parking areas provide access to various parts of the reserve, including short trails on the north side through Balblair Wood and along the flower-rich heath at Ferry Links from Littleferry.

◂ Loch Fleet from the Skelbo Road

Beinn Eighe Scottish Natural Heritage

Getting there Visitor centre (open Easter-Oct) on A832, 1km north of Kinlochewe. Self-guided trails at Glas Leitir, 4km north of Kinlochewe OS Map Landranger 19

Heavily forested on its lower slopes and with tundra-like conditions higher up, Beinn Eighe offers a vertical journey through a variety of life zones.

The massive scree slopes of Beinn Eighe epitomise the grandeur of a landscape where everything appears super sized: from the towering buttresses that glower across Loch Maree to the shattered quartzite ridges of the Beinn Eighe massif itself, this is upland terrain at its most imposing.

Today, the Beinn Eighe National Nature Reserve stretches from the southern shore of Loch Maree to the high ridges above Kinlochewe – although it was initially established in 1951 specifically to protect

Scotland's largest western fragment of old Caledonian forest.

Much of the effort focused on the woodland north of Kinlochewe at Glas Leitir, which includes a healthy mix of 'granny' pines – some more than 350 years old – and younger, straight-trunked specimens. Since the 1960s, the planting of additional Scots pine and other native species such as juniper, birch and rowan has replenished a mixed forest that now extends to an altitude of 300m.

Both pine marten and wildcat roam the woodland, but it takes a sharp eye – and a lot of luck – to spot them. Visitors are more likely to encounter Scottish crossbill and buzzard as well as the small numbers of roe deer that inhabit the woods. Red deer also shelter at the outer edges during harsh weather.

This particularly atmospheric forest can

Black-throated diver calling

Loch Maree divers

The densely forested islands on nearby Loch Maree provide a summer home for several pairs of black-throated diver, an elegant summer visitor to Highland lochs. Consummate performers in the water, divers are clumsy on land and so nest at the water's edge – leaving eggs vulnerable to fluctuations in water level. However, on Loch Maree, several pairs now nest on man-made platforms that are anchored to the loch bed and can rise and fall with any change in water level. The islands can be viewed from roadside vantage points, while summer boat trips operate from Loch Maree Hotel.

be explored using two circular paths: a relatively gentle woodland trail (1.5km) and a much tougher mountain trail (6.5km). Self-guided leaflets are available from the trailhead at the Glas Leitir car park.

While the woodland trail sticks to lower slopes, the mountain trail climbs through a variety of life zones – each with a distinctive climate, vegetation and wildlife – to an altitude of 550m.

Above 300m, the woodland starts to thin and is replaced by a cover of dwarf shrub heath comprised of stunted trees such as prostrate juniper. These hardy species – similar to those found on the Arctic tundra – are able to cope with the exposure, but eventually give way to bog, grassland and the naked rock terraces of the high plateau.

Golden eagle can sometimes be seen soaring above the treeline, while the summits also hold good numbers of ptarmigan. More reliable and certainly more vocal are the red deer that can make Beinn Eighe a noisy place during the October rut.

An SNH visitor centre north of Kinlochewe provides additional interpretation, while several trails provide access to the high tops.

◄ The Beinn Eighe massif from the mountain trail

Handa Island Scottish Wildlife Trust

Getting there **Boats depart daily (March-Sept, except Sundays) from Tarbet, 10km north of Scourie. Ferry charge**
OS Map **Landranger 9**

Dramatic upland scenery and up to 200,000 seabirds make Handa Island one of Scotland's most spectacular wildlife destinations.

Beautifully located just off the mainland, Handa's gently sloping southern shore is lapped by clear waters and dotted with sandy bays – one of which serves as the landing area for a small boat that ferries passengers across the sound from Tarbet.

One of the largest seabird stations in Britain, Handa serves as a valuable guide to the wider health of the marine environment in the Minch. Managed by SWT, all landing parties receive a brief orientation from the resident ranger before being directed to a 6km circular path that runs around the island.

Handa's interior has been colonised by great and Arctic skuas – both piratical species that harass other seabirds into dropping or disgorging their catch. Look for the noisy display of the thicker set great skuas (or bonxies), their wings raised to show off white patches beneath.

Formidable birds, both great and Arctic skuas are aggressive defenders of nest sites. A handful of attentive birds nest close to the raised boardwalk and will dive-bomb walkers if judged too close.

The moorland ends abruptly at towering cliffs at the north end of the island. Unlike the mainland, which is dominated by ancient Lewisian gneiss, Handa is comprised of

◀ Walkers pause on the raised boardwalk

Torridonian sandstone – a soft rock that has weathered perfectly to provide ledges for thousands of nesting seabirds. This includes Britain's largest colony of guillemots (150,000 individuals), plenty of razorbills (50,000), and a large population of fulmars, kittiwakes, shags and various gulls.

Much of the activity centres on the Great Stack, a freestanding pillar that holds a seething mass of nearly 10,000 guillemots on one face alone. Puffins also inhabit burrows on top of the stack, although some have begun to recolonise the main island following the eradication of rats. Handa's puffins are best seen opposite the Great Stack at its closest point to the main island.

But while the eradication of rats has benefited puffin and other species, almost all of Handa's seabirds now face a potentially greater challenge: lack of food. Although the Minch has traditionally been a reliable source of staples such as sprats and sandeels, recent seabird breeding failures – mirroring problems experienced elsewhere in Scotland – have caused serious concern.

Allow a minimum of three hours on the island, although an entire day can easily pass by. Boats shuttle back and forth from Tarbert on demand, starting at 9.30am and ending at 5pm.

Safety in numbers

The chocolate-brown guillemots that crowd the ledges along Handa's cliffs do so for good reason: breeding in such dense colonies provides extra vigilance against predators, while the social stimulation is designed to synchronise breeding efforts to coincide with good supplies of food. Given all the apparent confusion, it is hard to imagine how the adults identify their own egg and young. However, each guillemot egg has a distinct colour and pattern, while the chick calls to its parents for the several days it takes to chip its way out, so imprinting its call on the adult birds even before hatching.

Guillemot showing its yellow gape

Faraid Head

Getting there Park by Balnakeil House at end of minor road heading west on A838 from Durness OS Map Landranger 9

A narrow headland backed by a fine sandy beach, Faraid Head holds a small but easily accessible colony of puffins – despite the military manoeuvres nearby.

Jutting out nearly 4km into the Pentland Firth at the very roof of mainland Scotland, Faraid Head is typical of the landscape in this part of Sutherland: an alluring mix of cliffs, dunes and coastal grassland combine to create a range of specialist habitats for many plants and animals.

Faraid Head is accessed via Balnakeil Beach, a crescent-shaped stretch of sand backed by dunes and the kind of machair (flower-rich grassland) more commonly associated with Hebridean islands. Enriched by livestock grazing and wind-blown sand, the grassland is carpeted in orchids and many other flowering plants in summer.

Elsewhere, towards the end of the peninsula, outcrops of underlying Durness limestone also provide ideal soil conditions for even more specialist plant communities, including Scottish primrose.

However, the major draw at Faraid Head each summer is its scattering of puffin colonies; although not on such a grand scale as elsewhere in the region, the location and accessibility of the birds more than compensate for any lack of numbers.

Of the various colonies strung along the east of the headland, the easiest to reach is found just beyond Balnakeil Beach itself. Walk a few hundred metres along the road that rises from the beach and head right on a faint track that climbs gradually to a

Clo Mor cliffs

Incredibly, given the area's use as one of Europe's most active military bombardment ranges, the towering cliffs of Clo Mor near Cape Wrath hold vast numbers of seabirds, including a huge puffin colony. However, poor weather and frequent military operations mean that it can be a complex logistical exercise reaching the cliffs. In summer, most visitors cross the Kyle of Durness by passenger ferry and then use a connecting minibus service to travel the 19km to Cape Wrath. Others walk, cycle or use the minibus part way to access the cliffs. Check at the Durness Tourist Information Centre for ferry times and range operating hours.

viewpoint above a natural arch and surrounding stacks.

In a good season, around 200 pairs of puffin nest here. With care, sure-footed visitors can follow the old fence at the top of the cliff down to a small plateau overlooking the colony.

Puffins winter far out to sea, generally returning to Scottish breeding grounds in early April. Colonial breeders, the birds often use abandoned rabbit burrows as nest sites, although equipped with strong claws they are just as able to excavate their own tunnels.

A single egg is laid in May and, once hatched, each puffin chick remains within the relative safety of its grass-lined nest chamber. Most chicks leave their burrows in August, usually under cover of darkness to avoid predators such as skuas and larger gulls.

It is also possible to follow the coastline to the tip of Faraid Head where it ends at a small radar station now used as a control tower for the Ministry of Defence's nearby bombing range at Cape Wrath. Watching puffins at close quarters while fighter jets pound targets in the distance is an unusual – and somewhat unnerving – experience.

◄ Faraid Head and the distant cliffs of Clo Mor

Forsinard RSPB Reserve

Getting there On A897 northwest of Helmsdale, or by train from Inverness, Wick and Thurso. Visitor centre (open April–Oct) OS Map Landranger 17

A fragile habitat – part of the world's largest expanse of blanket bog – Forsinard sees an intense burst of wildlife activity in spring and summer.

The rolling peatland that covers large chunks of Caithness and Sutherland may look bleak, but represents a globally important environment: such habitat is found in only a handful of places around the world, and rarely does it cover such a vast area.

At Forsinard, the cool, maritime climate has created a waterlogged land of deer grass, moss and lichen.

Walking in a straight line here is almost impossible, although a little elevation is needed to appreciate why: the landscape – known since Viking times as the 'Flows' – contains a patchwork of dubh lochans.

The myriad pools sit on thick layers of peat that continue to grow at around one millimetre per year; the peat holds water so tightly that no two lochans have the same level of water. Many are linked at the bottom by peat pipes – mysterious tunnels sometimes used by otters to travel between pools.

Otters are typical of the wildlife at Forsinard in that they are reasonably plentiful, but tough to spot; the sheer size of the reserve means that wildlife watching requires patience – and timing.

Spring in the Flows brings a surge of activity, but arrives late this far north – May and June are the best times to visit. Arctic

Carnivorous plants such as butterwort (left) and sundew flourish in the bog

Peatland restoration

Although trees struggle to survive in the Flows naturally, it has not stopped people trying. Lured by attractive tax breaks in the 1980s, developers drained large areas for plantations of conifer and sitka spruce. The water table was lowered and parts of the bog dried out. Today, however, the RSPB is driving a long-term effort to convert afforested peatland back to blanket bog. This painstaking clearance of trees and unblocking of drains is one of the largest habitat restoration projects in Europe.

species such as red-throated divers return, while the Flows are also the summer home of a significant percentage of the UK's breeding common scoters.

In addition, the area is a haven for waders and is the UK stronghold for breeding greenshank. Birds of prey are equally plentiful: hen harriers return in May, while buzzard, merlin and even golden eagle can be spotted.

To avoid disturbance, visitors are asked not to stray onto the bog during the main breeding season (March-June), although wildlife can be just as easily enjoyed from the roadside. Between May and August, the RSPB operates twice-weekly guided walks across the bog.

For those going it alone, the croft land around Forsinain farm often has flocks of feeding waders (March-June) while greenshank are often seen along the Halladale river (April and May). Elsewhere, the public road from Kinbrice to Syre offers classic flow country views and a chance to spot the many red deer that roam the area.

An RSPB visitor centre in the old train station is manned from May until late August. Ask here about guided walks into less sensitive areas. Meanwhile, the nearby dubh lochan trail provides an easy journey across the bog and interpretation on the specialist plants and animals that survive in this formidable environment.

◀ Miles of moor at Forsinard

Index